◆ ANCIENT WORLD LEADERS ◆

ALEXANDER THE GREAT

ATTILA THE HUN

JULIUS CAESAR

CHARLEMAGNE

GENGHIS KHAN

SALADIN

ALEXANDER THE GREAT

◆◆◆

Samuel Willard Crompton

CHELSEA HOUSE
PUBLISHERS
A Haights Cross Communications ◆ Company

Philadelphia

Frontispiece: A depiction of Alexander the Great riding into battle. His immensely successful military record and his highly charismatic leadership paved the way for some of the greatest conquests the world has ever known, as well as spreading the Hellenistic civilization across Asia Minor.

CHELSEA HOUSE PUBLISHERS

VP, NEW PRODUCT DEVELOPMENT Sally Cheney
DIRECTOR OF PRODUCTION Kim Shinners
CREATIVE MANAGER Takeshi Takahashi
MANUFACTURING MANAGER Diann Grasse

Staff for ALEXANDER THE GREAT

ASSOCIATE EDITOR Benjamin Xavier Kim
PRODUCTION EDITOR Jaimie Winkler
PICTURE RESEARCHER Pat Holl
SERIES DESIGNER Takeshi Takahashi
COVER DESIGNER Takeshi Takahashi
LAYOUT 21st Century Publishing and Communications, Inc.

A Haights Cross Communications ◢ Company

http://www.chelseahouse.com

First Printing

1 3 5 7 9 8 6 4 2

Library of Congress Cataloging-in-Publication Data

Crompton, Samuel Willard.
  Alexander the Great / by Samuel Willard Crompton.
    p. cm.—(Ancient world leaders)
Summary: Describes the life and accomplishments of Alexander the Great of Macedonia. Includes bibliographical references and index.
  ISBN 0-7910-7219-3
  1. Alexander, the Great, 356–323 B.C.—Juvenile literature. 2. Greece—History—Macedonian Expansion, 359–323 B.C.—Juvenile literature. 3. Generals—Greece—Biography—Juvenile literature. 4. Greece—Kings and rulers—Biography—Juvenile literature. [1. Alexander, the Great, 356–323 B.C. 2. Kings, queens, rulers, etc. 3. Generals. 4. Greece—History—Macedonian Expansion, 359–323 B.C.] I. Title. II. Series.
DF234 .C72 2002
938'.07'092—dc21

2002151351

TABLE OF CONTENTS

Foreword: On Leadership
Arthur M. Schlesinger, jr.   6

1   Horse and Boy   12

2   From Pupil to Master   18

3   Greece and Persia   28

4   From the Hellespont to Issus   38

5   Egypt's New God   48

6   All the Treasures of the East   56

7   To the Ends of the World   64

8   The Waters of India   74

9   Perilous Journeys   80

10 The Price of Greatness   88

    Chronology   100

    Bibliography   102

    Further Reading   103

    Web Sites   104

    Index   105

ON LEADERSHIP

Arthur M. Schlesinger, jr.

Leadership, it may be said, is really what makes the world go round. Love no doubt smoothes the passage; but love is a private transaction between consenting adults. Leadership is a public transaction with history. The idea of leadership affirms the capacity of individuals to move, inspire, and mobilize masses of people so that they act together in pursuit of an end. Sometimes leadership serves good purposes, sometimes bad; but whether the end is benign or evil, great leaders are those men and women who leave their personal stamp on history.

Now, the very concept of leadership implies the proposition that individuals can make a difference. This proposition has never been universally accepted. From classical times to the present day, eminent thinkers have regarded individuals as no more than the agents and pawns of larger forces, whether the gods and goddesses of the ancient world or, in the modern era, race, class, nation, the dialectic, the will of the people, the spirit of the times, history itself. Against such forces, the individual dwindles into insignificance.

So contends the thesis of historical determinism. Tolstoy's great novel *War and Peace* offers a famous statement of the case. Why, Tolstoy asked, did millions of men in the Napoleonic Wars, denying their human feelings and their common sense, move back and forth across Europe slaughtering their fellows? "The war," Tolstoy answered, "was bound to happen simply because it was bound to happen." All prior history determined it. As for leaders, they, Tolstoy said, "are but the labels that serve to give a name to an end and, like labels, they have the least possible connection with the event." The greater the leader, "the more conspicuous the inevitability and the predestination of every act he commits." The leader, said Tolstoy, is "the slave of history."

Determinism takes many forms. Marxism is the determinism of class. Nazism the determinism of race. But the idea of men and women as the slaves of history runs athwart the deepest human instincts. Rigid determinism abolishes the idea of human freedom—the assumption of free choice that underlies every move we make, every word we speak, every thought we think. It abolishes the idea of human responsibility, since it is manifestly unfair to reward or punish people for actions that are by definition beyond their control. No one can live consistently by any deterministic creed. The Marxist states prove this themselves by their extreme susceptibility to the cult of leadership.

More than that, history refutes the idea that individuals make no difference. In December 1931 a British politician crossing Fifth Avenue in New York City between 76th and 77th Streets around 10:30 P.M. looked in the wrong direction and was knocked down by an automobile—a moment, he later recalled, of a man aghast, a world aglare: "I do not understand why I was not broken like an eggshell or squashed like a gooseberry." Fourteen months later an American politician, sitting in an open car in Miami, Florida, was fired on by an assassin; the man beside him was hit. Those who believe that individuals make no difference to history might well ponder whether the next two decades would have been the same had Mario Constasino's car killed Winston Churchill in 1931 and Giuseppe Zangara's bullet killed Franklin Roosevelt in 1933. Suppose, in addition, that Lenin had died of typhus in Siberia in 1895 and that Hitler had been killed on the western front in 1916. What would the 20th century have looked like now?

For better or for worse, individuals do make a difference. "The notion that a people can run itself and its affairs anonymously," wrote the philosopher William James, "is now well known to be the silliest of absurdities. Mankind does nothing save through initiatives on the part of inventors, great or small, and imitation by the rest of us—these are the sole factors in human progress. Individuals of genius show the way, and set the patterns, which common people then adopt and follow."

Leadership, James suggests, means leadership in thought as well as in action. In the long run, leaders in thought may well make the greater difference to the world. "The ideas of economists and political philosophers, both when they are right and when they are wrong," wrote John Maynard Keynes, "are more powerful than is commonly understood. Indeed the world is ruled by little else. Practical men, who believe themselves to be quite exempt from any intellectual influences, are usually the slaves of some defunct economist. . . . The power of vested interests is vastly exaggerated compared with the gradual encroachment of ideas."

But, as Woodrow Wilson once said, "Those only are leaders of men, in the general eye, who lead in action. . . . It is at their hands that new thought gets its translation into the crude language of deeds." Leaders in thought often invent in solitude and obscurity, leaving to later generations the tasks of imitation. Leaders in action—the leaders portrayed in this series—have to be effective in their own time.

And they cannot be effective by themselves. They must act in response to the rhythms of their age. Their genius must be adapted, in a phrase from William James, "to the receptivities of the moment." Leaders are useless without followers. "There goes the mob," said the French politician, hearing a clamor in the streets. "I am their leader. I must follow them." Great leaders turn the inchoate emotions of the mob to purposes of their own. They seize on the opportunities of their time, the hopes, fears, frustrations, crises, potentialities. They succeed when events have prepared the way for them, when the community is awaiting to be aroused, when they can provide the clarifying and organizing ideas. Leadership completes the circuit between the individual and the mass and thereby alters history.

It may alter history for better or for worse. Leaders have been responsible for the most extravagant follies and most monstrous crimes that have beset suffering humanity. They have also been vital in such gains as humanity has made in individual freedom, religious and racial tolerance, social justice, and respect for human rights.

There is no sure way to tell in advance who is going to lead for good and who for evil. But a glance at the gallery of men and women in ANCIENT WORLD LEADERS suggests some useful tests.

One test is this: Do leaders lead by force or by persuasion? By command or by consent? Through most of history leadership was exercised by the divine right of authority. The duty of followers was to defer and to obey. "Theirs not to reason why/Theirs but to do and die." On occasion, as with the so-called enlightened despots of the 18th century in Europe, absolutist leadership was animated by humane purposes. More often, absolutism nourished the passion for domination, land, gold, and conquest and resulted in tyranny.

The great revolution of modern times has been the revolution of equality. "Perhaps no form of government," wrote the British historian James Bryce in his study of the United States, *The American Commonwealth*, "needs great leaders so much as democracy." The idea that all people should be equal in their legal condition has undermined the old structure of authority, hierarchy, and deference. The revolution of equality has had two contrary effects on the nature of leadership. For equality, as Alexis de Tocqueville pointed out in his great study *Democracy in America*, might mean equality in servitude as well as equality in freedom.

"I know of only two methods of establishing equality in the political world," Tocqueville wrote. "Rights must be given to every citizen, or none at all to anyone . . . save one, who is the master of all." There was no middle ground "between the sovereignty of all and the absolute power of one man." In his astonishing prediction of 20th-century totalitarian dictatorship, Tocqueville explained how the revolution of equality could lead to the *Führerprinzip* and more terrible absolutism than the world had ever known.

But when rights are given to every citizen and the sovereignty of all is established, the problem of leadership takes a new form, becomes more exacting than ever before. It is easy to issue commands and enforce them by the rope and the stake, the concentration camp and the *gulag*. It is much harder to use argument and achievement to overcome opposition and win consent. The Founding Fathers of the United States understood the difficulty. They believed that history had given them the opportunity to decide, as Alexander Hamilton wrote in the first Federalist Paper, whether men are indeed capable of basing government on "reflection and choice, or whether they are forever destined to depend . . . on accident and force."

Government by reflection and choice called for a new style of leadership and a new quality of followership. It required leaders to be responsive to popular concerns, and it required followers to be active and informed participants in the process. Democracy does not eliminate emotion from politics; sometimes it fosters demagoguery; but it is confident that, as the greatest of democratic leaders put it, you cannot fool all of the people all of the time. It measures leadership by results and retires those who overreach or falter or fail.

It is true that in the long run despots are measured by results too. But they can postpone the day of judgment, sometimes indefinitely, and in the meantime they can do infinite harm. It is also true that democracy is no guarantee of virtue and intelligence in government, for the voice of the people is not necessarily the voice of God. But democracy, by assuring the right of opposition, offers built-in resistance to the evils inherent in absolutism. As the theologian Reinhold Niebuhr summed it up, "Man's capacity for justice makes democracy possible, but man's inclination to justice makes democracy necessary."

A second test for leadership is the end for which power is sought. When leaders have as their goal the supremacy of a master race or the promotion of totalitarian revolution or the acquisition and exploitation of colonies or the protection of greed and privilege or the preservation of personal power, it is likely that their leadership will do little to advance the cause of humanity. When their goal is the abolition of slavery, the liberation of women, the enlargement of opportunity for the poor and powerless, the extension of equal rights to racial minorities, the defense of the freedoms of expression and opposition, it is likely that their leadership will increase the sum of human liberty and welfare.

Leaders have done great harm to the world. They have also conferred great benefits. You will find both sorts in this series. Even "good" leaders must be regarded with a certain wariness. Leaders are not demigods; they put on their trousers one leg after another just like ordinary mortals. No leader is infallible, and every leader needs to be reminded of this at regular intervals. Irreverence irritates leaders but is their salvation. Unquestioning submission corrupts leaders and demeans followers. Making a cult of a leader is always a mistake. Fortunately hero worship generates its own antidote. "Every hero," said Emerson, "becomes a bore at last."

The single benefit the great leaders confer is to embolden the rest of us to live according to our own best selves, to be active, insistent, and resolute in affirming our own sense of things. For great leaders attest to the reality of human freedom against the supposed inevitabilities of history. And they attest to the wisdom and power that may lie within the most unlikely of us, which is why Abraham Lincoln remains the supreme example of great leadership. A great leader, said Emerson, exhibits new possibilities to all humanity. "We feed on genius . . . . Great men exist that there may be greater men."

Great leaders, in short, justify themselves by emancipating and empowering their followers. So humanity struggles to master its destiny, remembering with Alexis de Tocqueville: "It is true that around every man a fatal circle is traced beyond which he cannot pass; but within the wide verge of that circle he is powerful and free; as it is with man, so with communities." ▪

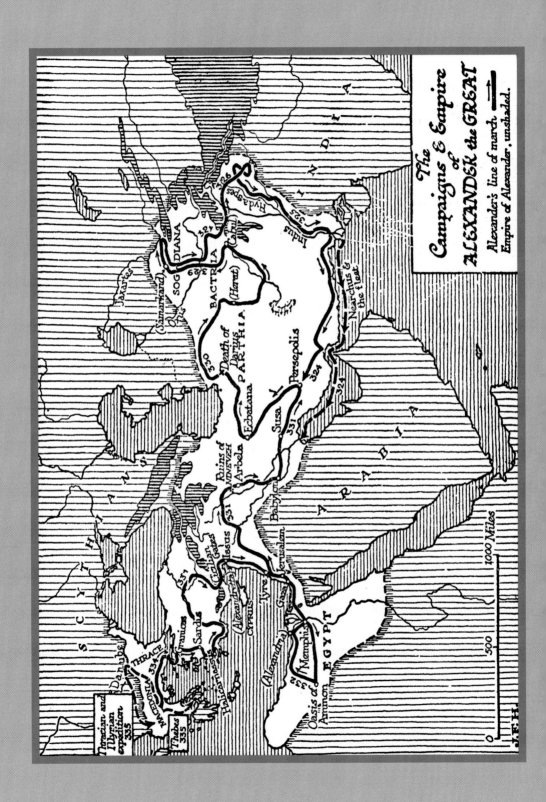

The Campaigns & Empire of ALEXANDER the GREAT

Alexander's line of march ———▶
Empire of Alexander, unshaded.

1000 Miles
0   500

J.F.H.

INDIA

SCYTHIANS

SOGDIANA
(Samarkand)
Oxus
329
328
BACTRIA
(Herat)
PARTHIA
Death of
Darius
330
Ecbatana

Hydaspes
326
(Cabul)
Indus
325
Nearchus &
the fleet

Persepolis
324
Susa
331
324

ARABIA

Ruins of
NINEVEH
Arbela

Babylon
331
Jerusalem
Gaza
Tyre
331
Cilician Gates
Issus
331
(Alexandria)
Cyprus

Alexandria
332
Memphis
Oasis of
Ammon

EGYPT

Danube
THRACE
334
MACEDONIA
(Thebes)
335
Granicus
334
Sardis
Halicarnassus

Thracian and
Illyrian expedition
335

1

HORSE
AND BOY

On a fine spring day, around the year 345 B.C., King Philip of
Macedon took his son Alexander to meet a horse trader from
nearby Thessaly. Macedonians loved horses, and the Thessalians had
access both to the horses from Greece and from abroad because of
their proximity to the Aegean Sea. Among the horses for sale was one
named Bucephalus, which means "bull head." He had a prominent
mark on his head, and his head was shaped more like a bull than a
horse. The horse trader put Bucephalus up for sale, but he warned
King Philip that this horse was exceedingly hard to master. He was
about 12 years old and had never been properly broken in because of
his wild and powerful spirit.

Words of warning would actually do little to dissuade the
Macedonians, for they loved challenges. One by one, King Philip's
best riders came forth and attempted to master Bucephalus. One
by one, they were either thrown off, or could not mount the horse

A sculpture depicts one of the first moments in Alexander's life that foretold how successful he would be in attaining goals in the future—the taming of the horse Bucephalus, which had thrown off other horsemen before Alexander claimed he could tame it.

in the first place. Then came a shout:

"What a horse they are losing! And all because they are too inexperienced and feeble to manage him!"

Even though he was the prince, Alexander's outburst was completely out of line. He was speaking of Macedonian horsemen, the best known in the Western world.

King Philip admonished his son, saying, "Who are you to criticize your elders? Do you think you know more than them, or can manage horses better?"

A different type of prince might have accepted the reprimand. Alexander, however, had been raised to take any challenge. He replied, "Yes, I do think I could manage *this* horse better than others have done."

By now looks were exchanged between the King and his courtiers.

"If you don't succeed in doing so, what penalty are you prepared to pay for your cheek [insolence]?" asked King Philip.

"I guarantee to pay the price of the horse," responded Alexander.

Philip gestured to Alexander to take the opportunity. Alexander went up to Bucephalus and turned him in a different direction. By guiding the horse, Alexander turned Bucephalas away from the sunlight. Alexander had seen that the horse was frightened by the appearance of his shadow; by turning in a different direction, Alexander removed the shadow, and some of the horse's fear dissipated.

Murmuring soft words, Alexander first walked and then ran with the horse. Finally, at a moment when he could see that the horse was ready to ride, Alexander leapt up and sat astride Bucephalus. Once he was aloft, Alexander had to hold on tight, for the horse had a fiery spirit. But Alexander kept his seat, and the crowning moment came when he managed to persuade Bucephalus to turn and change direction; Alexander had mastered the horse.

The historian Plutarch, to whom we owe most of the details of this extraordinary moment, relates that when Alexander cantered the horse back to where Philip and his men stood, the king's eyes filled with tears. Philip exclaimed,

"Son, you had better try to find a kingdom you fit: Macedonia is too small for you!"

Some men are born to conquer, while some are born

to inspire and motivate. Alexander had all three qualities. Bucephalus was not only Alexander's first conquest, but became one of the prince's lifelong friends. They would share the next 18 years together and would travel from Macedonia to India in each other's company.

Alexander, the Prince of Macedon, was born sometime in 356 B.C. His father was Philip II, King of Macedonia, and his mother was Olympias, a princess from Epirus, which was located in what is present-day Albania.

Philip and Olympias had a passionate, stormy relationship. Philip loved Olympias, but believed she should simply accept that he would have affairs and other wives. Olympias, having been raised a princess, thought this was absurd. Adding to her pride, Olympias was a leader in the cult of the Greek god Dionysus. Given her royal station and her participation in religious ceremonies, she felt that Philip's having other wives meant both personal abandonment and disrespect to the god she served.

Philip and Olympias were both prideful, a factor that had helped to draw them together at the start. But within two years of Alexander's birth, King Philip began to have affairs with other women. Queen Olympias was first upset, then furious. Increasingly she drew her son close to her, and began to whisper things in his ear. One of her messages was that Philip was not his true father—that Alexander had been fathered by one of the gods. Relations between Philip and Olympias only grew worse as Alexander grew older. One can truly say that he grew up in a deeply dysfunctional family.

Alexander grew up in Pella, the Macedonian capital. Pella was a rude city by Greek standards; it lacked the sophistication and elegance of Greek cities like Athens, Thebes, and Corinth. If anything, Pella was rather like Sparta, capital city of the Spartans, who were known for their rejection of comfort. In fact, the word "spartan" still means sparse, masculine, without anything extra.

Alexander was born to King Philip and Queen Olympias, but as his parents' marriage began to unravel, the two parents would jockey for control of Alexander's life. From an early age, Olympias would tell Alexander that he was actually descended from the gods, which may have instilled in him a sense of divine right—or superiority over his fellow man.

King Philip, Queen Olympias, and Prince Alexander all knew that the Greeks to the south looked down on Macedonia. According to the Athenians, Thebans, Corinthians, and even the Spartans, Macedonia was a wild, uncivilized place, fit only for horsemen and shepherds. Though father, mother, and son had many differences of opinion, and often quarreled, they were united in one thing: their desire to see Macedonia attain glory.

Philip had spent several years as a hostage in the Greek city-state of Thebes. There Philip had seen both the power of the city-states and the weakness caused by their rivalries with one another. As an adult king, Philip emulated some of the military tactics he had observed at Thebes. Philip's greatest desire was to master all of Greece—to have the numerous city-states submit to his will.

Alexander's parents were estranged, and each of them expected, or rather demanded, different things from him. Philip wanted his son to demonstrate that he was courageous and ambitious, while Olympias wanted her son to show that he was descended from the gods.

Tormented by the conflicts between his parents, Alexander found an important outlet in the company of the ordinary Macedonian soldiers. From an early age he was their favorite. The soldiers admired Philip for his foresight and inspired leadership, but they loved Alexander for the simplicity of his needs and his desire to share their life with all its hardships. Alexander showed a disdain for physical comfort; he preferred the rough-and-tumble life of the Macedonian soldiers. From these Macedonian soldiers, Alexander learned of his own charisma, setting him on course to becoming a leader that others believed in.

FROM PUPIL
TO MASTER

Not long after Alexander broke in Bucephalus, King Philip found a new tutor for his promising son. Though he was a tough Macedonian, Philip knew the advantages that could be gained from acquaintance with Greek knowledge. The king hired the philosopher Aristotle of Athens to come to Pella and teach Prince Alexander.

At this time, Aristotle was not yet the most famous mind of his generation. Born in Stagira on the same peninsula as Mount Athos, Aristotle had spent his adult life in Athens. He was the pupil of Plato, who had been the pupil of Socrates. Therefore, Aristotle was the recipient of the best one-on-one education that the classical world had to offer. To this he added a new and more practical emphasis.

Aristotle had prior connections with the Macedonian court. His father Nicomachus had been physician to King Amyntas, Philip's father, and Alexander's grandfather. In 344 B.C., King Philip and Aristotle came to terms. Aristotle was not averse to teaching the

Seeking only the best education for his son, King Philip arranged a deal with the Greek philosopher Aristotle to come to Macedonia and teach Alexander personally. While the two did not always see eye-to-eye on various things, there is no doubt that Aristotle's teachings had a profound influence on the young prince's life.

Macedonian prince—far from it. The philosopher recognized a great opportunity to help shape the mind and character of a future ruler. But Aristotle's primary condition was that King Philip restore the town and people of Stagira. Located on the northeast side of Macedonia, the town had been ravaged in one of Philip's many wars. In return for Aristotle's agreement to tutor Prince Alexander, King Philip had the town rebuilt and as many of its former citizens as possible returned to their place of origin.

Aristotle arrived at Pella sometime in 344 B.C. Philip wanted Alexander and the other court pages taught in a different location, away from Queen Olympias. Therefore Philip created a school at Mieza, one day's journey west of Pella. The establishment of the school, and Alexander's placement there, were all part of Philip's efforts to work Alexander away from Olympias' influence.

No record exists of the subjects that Aristotle taught, or of the method of instruction. This is unfortunate, since with a record we would today have a much better understanding of the extent to which Aristotle shaped his young pupil. By looking at Aristotle's achievements to that date, however, we can surmise something of what was taught at Mieza.

Aristotle had already proved himself a master of observation. He had learned more, and written more, about the life and migration of birds than any previous scientist of the ancient world. Aristotle knew a great deal about geography and the cultural associations of many peoples from around the Mediterranean world; his knowledge in this regard came primarily from the Greek historian Herodotus. Given Aristotle's interest in the development of logic, one can assume that this would also have formed an important element in Alexander's studies.

Aristotle later wrote two books that he dedicated to Prince Alexander: *Monarchy* and *On Colonies*. Both books hint at strains that developed in the relationship between the middle-aged philosopher and the teenage prince. In *Monarchy*, Aristotle went so far as to say that absolute monarchy was valuable only when the ruler's intelligence transcended the intelligence of his subjects to the same degree that human intelligence transcends animal intelligence. In *On Colonies*, Aristotle rejected what would become one of the hallmarks of Alexander's policy. Aristotle believed that Greeks (and by extension Macedonians)

were so superior to other peoples—the Persians in particular—
that no effort should be made to bring the peoples together,
and that the Greeks should remain aloof. This, however, would
not be Alexander's policy.

Years later, Aristotle also wrote a long letter to Alexander on
the subject of Rhetoric (speechmaking). The lengthy document
began with an admonition to Alexander to make his speaking
style the best that it could be, saying, "Just as you are desirous
to have more splendid raiment than other men, so you ought
to strive to attain to a more glorious skill in speech than
other men possess. For it is far more honourable and kingly
to have the mind well ordered than to see the bodily form
well arrayed."

Alexander appears to have taken this lesson to heart. Years
later, when he was on campaign in the Middle East and Persia,
he would be able to rouse his men to greater exertions and
greater sacrifices than any other leader of his time.

Alexander's studies came to a rather abrupt end sometime
in 340 B.C. This was not because King Philip was dissatisfied
with Aristotle or his teachings, but because Philip went away
on a campaign to the north. In his absence, Philip made the
16-year-old Alexander his regent. Suddenly, the boy had
become a temporary monarch.

Soon after Philip returned from his northern campaign, he
found that the Greeks were joining against him. Inspired by the
Athenian orator Demosthenes, Athens and Thebes had formed
an alliance against Philip and Macedonia. Demosthenes spoke so
often and so violently against Philip that the word "Philippic"
in our language today means an intemperate personal attack on
a political rival.

Given the hindsight of history, it is easy to see that Philip
would defeat the Thebans and Athenians. During nearly 20
years on the throne, Philip had shaped the Macedonian army
into a new and improved fighting force. The core was still
the *phalanx*, consisting of soldiers who locked shields and

advanced brandishing their 16-foot-long spears. Philip had altered the cavalry component, making it both larger and faster. The King's Companions, as they were called, were the shock troops, intended to hit the enemy as it recoiled from the advance of the phalanx. On top of it all, the Macedonian army had in Philip a leader of true brilliance who would adapt to any situation and make the best of it.

Philip and Alexander went south to meet the enemy. This journey and campaign was one of the major testing and turning points of their relationship. Would Alexander prove to be the type of son worthy to succeed Philip?

Philip's Macedonian army met the men of Athens and Thebes at Charonea in 338 B.C. The battle was nearly a draw, but a charge by the King's Companions, led by Prince Alexander, won the day. The Sacred Band of Thebes—a hard-core group of 330 men, devoted and sworn to one another—perished to a man. Philip had won the battle, and with it, most of Greece. Only Sparta continued to resist Philip as overlord of Greece after the Battle of Chareonea.

Granted the title of *hegemon* (or leader) of Greece, Philip returned north to Macedonia. His intentions were already plain; having subdued Greece, he wanted to invade Asia Minor, the furthest extension of the great Persian Empire. To many, Philip's idea seemed the height of *hubris* (pride and folly). Philip had spent years developing the Macedonian army into a tight-knit unit, and he believed the Macedonians would follow him into Asia.

Just one year after his greatest triumph, Philip decided to take a new bride. There was nothing surprising in this, as Philip was of a very amorous nature, and he believed it was his privilege as King of Macedonia to take as many wives as he desired. But Queen Olympias was furious, and she vowed to take revenge on the new wife, Cleopatra. The name "Cleopatra" was actually prevalent in Macedonian society for centuries before the appearance of the famed Cleopatra of

The *phalanx* formed the core of the Macedonian army, a group of soldiers who locked shields and marched with their long spears held outward—effectively becoming a deadly and impenetrable mobile wall. The phalanx, in addition to the cavalry, made the Macedonian army one of the best in the known world.

Egypt. In fact, Cleopatra of Egypt would be a descendant of one of Alexander's best generals.

Making matters even worse, Philip then decided to marry his daughter—also named Cleopatra, and who was two years younger than Alexander—to Olympias' brother, Alexander of Epirus. Not only was the marriage incestuous, but it would serve to diminish Olympias' standing at court even further.

Now Olympias' fury truly knew no bounds.

On the day of the wedding between Cleopatra and her uncle, Philip was stabbed and killed by a Macedonian courtier. Little is known of the assassin, but it seems very likely he was either a follower of Olympias or someone she had hired. In either case, Philip was dead. The marriage between Cleopatra and her uncle Alexander was of no consequence, and Alexander, the Prince of Macedonia, became its king in 336 B.C.

Alexander ensured that Philip's assassin would receive dire and dreaded punishment which led to death. Philip and his wife Cleopatra—whom Olympias had forced to commit suicide—were both buried at Aigira, a former Macedonian capital. Their remains were uncovered in 1977 and since have been positively confirmed.

Prince Alexander was now king. How would he perform in this new post?

Many Athenians, Thebans, Spartans, and other Greeks rejoiced to learn of Philip's death. No one, they reasoned, could be as bad for them as Philip had been. His son was only 20 years old. Rather little was known of him, except that he had played the flute and lyre from an early age. Surely he would be easier to manage than Philip had been. Perhaps the Greek city-states would overthrow Macedonian rule and go their separate ways once more.

All the Greek city-states showed resistance to Macedonian rule, but Thebes was in the forefront. Just 20 years earlier, Thebes had been the preeminent military power in Greece; her leaders wanted to reclaim that role. So, when the Greek revolt against Alexander began, Thebes led the way.

Alexander led the Macedonian army south, just as he and his father had done three years earlier. The difference was that instead of the veteran Philip as leader, the Macedonian army was led by a 20-year-old, which gave more hope to the men of Thebes.

Alexander arrived at the gates of Thebes and laid siege to the ancient city. By a ruse, his men managed to get inside the gates and take over the city. Now could have been a time to be merciful, for the revolt had caused little damage to Alexander or his reputation. Alexander was vengeful. He ordered the destruction of the city and for its inhabitants to be sold into slavery. Over 30,000 people lost their homes, their families, and their freedom because of Alexander's decision. Only one house he spared, because it belonged to the poet Pindar, whom he admired.

After the destruction of Thebes, every city-state hastened to send messages of submission. Alexander had become master of Greece in a way that his father had not been, but Alexander's accomplishment was also very much based on Philip's earlier work. Alexander went on to Athens. In the neighborhood of that great city, Alexander met the philosopher Diogenes, who was proud of his lack of reliance on material possessions or comforts. Alexander met Diogenes on the street, where the philosopher spent his days. Standing over the poet, Alexander inquired what he might do for Diogenes. The answer came back, swift and sure:

"Move a little bit. You are blocking the sunlight."

That was the substance of the conversation. As they left Diogenes where they had found him, Alexander's courtiers abused the old man, pointing out his folly. But Alexander said quietly,

"As for me, if I were not Alexander, I would be Diogenes."

Alexander returned to Pella soon after his meeting with Diogenes. Though he would bring Greek civilization to much of Asia, Alexander was never truly comfortable in the Greek city-states. He remained a man of the mountains, of Pella, and of Macedonia.

Within a few months of his return to Pella, Alexander

In the city of Athens, Alexander met the ascetic philosopher Diogenes. Alexander asked if there was anything that he could do for the old man. Diogenes replied, "Move a little bit. You are blocking the sunlight." Though Alexander's men reprimanded Diogenes for being impudent, Alexander admired the philosopher's simple requirements for life.

had developed his plans for a new military campaign. He intended to fulfill the ambition of his father and invade the Persian Empire.

Knowing that he would be absent a long time, Alexander turned to Antipater, one of his father's most trusted generals, and made him regent. Antipater would rule for Alexander as long as the true king was away. Alexander and Antipater maintained good relations throughout Alexander's lifetime, but it was a different story with Cassander, Antipater's son. Cassander and Alexander had been bitter rivals in their youth. Alexander now purposefully left Cassander in Macedonia; he did not want a rival to stick thorns into his side during the great campaign that lay ahead. Alexander did take Callisthenes, who was a relative of Aristotle. Alexander also promised to send samples of the plants and flowers he encountered back to his old teacher.

As Alexander gathered his men and prepared to cross into Asia Minor, he must have recollected the long history of conflict between Greece and Persia. He had read Homer, Herodotus, and Xexophon. Now he would cross the Hellespont into Asia and make history himself.

GREECE AND PERSIA

After he subdued Thebes, Alexander turned his gaze eastward to Asia Minor and Persia. Though the Greeks and Persians had been enemies for more than 150 years, the two peoples knew rather little of each other. Were it not for the writings of Xenophon, Alexander would know even less than he did about the great empire to the east.

Persian history begins with the life and reign of Cyrus II, better known as Cyrus the Great. Cyrus is the Greek transliteration of *Kurash* which means "shepherd." Cyrus probably never tended sheep, but as the leader of the Persians he was considered their great shepherd. Seldom have a name and a man been so well-matched.

Born around 580 B.C., Cyrus was the son of Cambyses, a local lord in the area known as Parshan. This area was located in the southern part of what is now Iran. It is a hot, dusty region, with refuge from the heat found only in the mountains. There Cyrus was born and raised.

Cyrus the Great was the ruler of Persia who united the Persian and Median tribes. This combined force provided a powerful army which conquered many neighbors, making the Persian Empire one of the largest in the world. Here King Croesus of Lycia, whom Cyrus defeated in 545 B.C., is shown before the Persian ruler.

The Persians were a hardy people, just a few generations removed from nomadic status. Like all Persian boys, Cyrus knew the axiom concerning adulthood. For a boy to become a Persian man, he had to ride a horse well, shoot an arrow straight, and tell the truth.

Sometime around 550 B.C., Cyrus united the Persians and Medes. Both were groups of Iranian tribesmen, but the Medes were more sophisticated and advanced than their cousins. The Medes had helped overthrow the oppressive Assyrian Empire around 612 B.C. and since had ruled in splendor from their capital of Ecbatana. Somehow, Cyrus brought together two groups of horse-warrior peoples and united them into one of the great forces of world history.

It is not certain whether Cyrus was a military genius or a unifier and administrator of the highest rank. Perhaps he was both. In either case, he led the Persians and Medes to stunning victories over their neighbors. In 545 B.C., Cyrus defeated King Croesus of Lydia in what is now Turkey. By doing so, Cyrus gained the great wealth that Croesus had gathered (even today, the expression "as rich as Croesus" holds weight).

Cyrus went on to conquer the Babylonians. He entered Babylon in 538 B.C. He was now the master of most of the area known as the Fertile Crescent, stretching from the eastern parts of Turkey to the Persian Gulf. Cyrus insisted that he had come as a liberator. He declared, "I, Cyrus, will gather together all those peoples and restore them to their homes."

These were not just words. Cyrus freed numerous peoples who had been brought to Babylon as captives and slaves. Among those freed were the Hebrews, who had been brought to Babylon in 587 B.C. by King Nebuchadnezzar. Nebuchadnezzar had destroyed the great temple built by Solomon around 1000 B.C. Now Cyrus freed the Hebrews and allowed them to return home.

The Old Testament portrays Cyrus as a man of God, sent to free the Hebrews: "In the first year of the Persian king, Cyrus, the Lord fulfilled the promise which he had made through Jeremias. He put a new resolve into the heart of Cyrus, king of Persia, who thereupon published a written decree all through his dominions." Cyrus not only freed the Hebrews, but he sent them back to Jerusalem so they could rebuild the great temple, a project that took about twenty years. (This second one lasted until the Romans destroyed it in 70 A.D.)

Cyrus was now at the peak of his powers. Known as the "King of Kings" and ruler of the four quarters of the Earth, he controlled more land than any monarch before him. Under his rule were Babylonians, Lydians, former Assyrians, Chaldeans, Bactrians, Phoenicians, and Hebrews. Cyrus wanted to conquer Egypt as a way of rounding out his successes. But first he went to the northeastern part of his empire to fight against tribes known as the Sarmatians and Massagetae. Cyrus met his death in one of those border fights; legend has it that he was killed by a woman named Tymiris, one of the leaders of the Massagetae. Cyrus' body was brought back to his homeland of Parsha. He was buried in a rather simple tomb at Parsagard (which Alexander would later visit).

Cambyses was Cyrus' son and heir. Cambyses completed his father's work and conquered Egypt, going to its southern regions—farther than almost any outsider had done. When Cambyses fell ill and died in Egypt, the throne passed to a distant kinsman known as Darius.

Darius the First (usually known as Darius the Great) continued the expansion of the Persian Empire. Darius built upon the achievements of Cyrus and upon those of the Medes who were co-rulers of the empire. Median craftsmen shaped and fashioned the beautiful Persian palaces that arose at Susa and Persepolis. The former Median capital of Ecbatana became the summer palace of the Persian leaders, who would then go north to escape the summer heat at Persepolis.

During Darius' years on the throne, the Persian Empire was knit together in a way that has seldom been equaled until our current day. To inform the King of Kings what happened in any part of the empire, the Persians developed a series of couriers who rode horseback and delivered messages that were handed over to new sets of riders. It was said that a message could pass from the former kingdom of Lydia in Asia Minor to Susa in eight days of hard riding; by contrast, the trip on foot or by mule would take over three months! The Greek historian Herodotus

Darius the Great ruled the Persian empire after Cyrus, and during his reign the Persians and the Greeks came into contact with each other for the first time, ending with the Persians' defeat at Marathon. It was not to be the last conflict between the two great civilizations.

described these riders and their devotion, writing, "Nothing stops these couriers from covering their allotted stage in the quickest possible time—neither snow, rain, heat, nor darkness. The first, at the end of his stage, passes the dispatch to the second, the second to the third, and so on along the line, as in the Greek torch race which is held in honour of Hephasteus."

The United States Postal Service today uses an adaptation of Herodotus' words for its motto: "Neither rain, nor snow, nor heat, nor gloom of night stays these couriers from the swift completion of their appointed rounds."

Toward the end of his long and successful reign, Darius learned of a revolt in one of the most distant of his provinces on the western coast of Asia Minor (which is now Turkey). Darius sent forces to subdue the revolt there, and in so doing, he came into conflict with the Greeks for the first time.

The Greek city-states of Athens, Thebes, Corinth, Sparta, and elsewhere had developed in isolation from Persia. The Greeks had a long tradition of self-government. They had not been part of either the Egyptian or Babylonian empires, and they did not wish to become part of the Persian one. So when Darius sent ambassadors to Greece, demanding that the people there show their submission by offering earth and water, the Spartans threw the ambassadors into a well where they died. The war was on.

In 490 B.C., Darius sent a fleet and army from Asia Minor. The King of Kings was not on the expedition, entrusting command to one of his generals. The Persians landed on a beach called Marathon, about 25 miles northeast of Athens.

The Greeks did not have the horse-riding courier system of the Persians. Instead the Greeks relied on swift-footed men who carried messages from one city-state to another. In 490 B.C., the Athenians sent a runner named Pheidippides to Sparta. He covered the 150 miles in a few days and then returned with bad news: the Spartans would not move until the moon was full. Pheidippides then joined the Athenian army overlooking the plain of Marathon.

The Athenians and Thebans had gathered their men on a rocky headland overlooking the plain of Marathon. There were ten Athenian and Theban generals that day. They voted as to their course of action and decided on a downhill charge against the Persians.

The men of Athens and Thebes leveled their spears and charged onto the plain at Marathon. The Greek warriors, called *hoplites*, wore light armor and held spears. The Persians who met them on the beach wore leather and carried axes and swords, rather than spears. It was the first clash between the two peoples, who came from such different places and who held such different philosophies. The Greek historian Herodotus described the moment:

"They were the first Greeks, so far as we know, to charge at a run, and the first who dared to look without flinching at Persian dress and the men who wore it; for until that day came, no Greek could even hear the word Persian without terror."

The Greeks won the day in a resounding fashion. Over 6,000 Persians were killed on the beach; the others escaped to their ships. News of the victory was brought to Athens by Pheidippides. He had fought in the battle and then ran 26 miles back to the city. Pheidippides died immediately after bursting through the city gate and delivering the news. The modern "marathon" of 26 miles comes from his dramatic run.

Athens and Thebes held major victory celebrations. The Spartan warriors, who arrived late, had to go home without having won any laurels.

Darius the First (Darius the Great) died in 486 B.C. The throne went to his son Xerxes, who planned a major invasion of Greece to avenge the defeat at Marathon.

Xerxes sent couriers and messages to all parts of the vast Persian Empire. When he marched across Asia Minor in the spring of 480 B.C., Xerxes led approximately 300,000 men, drawn from as far away as Bactria and Gedrosia. The Persians crossed the Hellespont, the body of water between Asia Minor and Europe, by building a bridge of boats. Once across, the vast Persian army headed south and west, aiming to subdue all of Greece.

This time the Spartans responded in time. King Leonidas led 300 Spartans to a narrow mountain pass called Thermopylae. The pass was the way to the Attic peninsula and Athens. If they could hold this pass, the Spartans would redeem their absence at Marathon.

Xerxes and his Persians came to the mountain pass. The Spartans guarded an area so narrow that no more than three men could pass. For several days Xerxes hurled his men against the Spartans. Even the "Immortals," Xerxes' 10,000-man elite bodyguard, could not force their way through. It was only when a Greek turned traitor that the Persians learned of another path that would bring them on the other side of the

Spartans. With this knowledge, the Persian surrounded and then killed the 300 Spartans. King Leonidas and his men lay dead. This had cost the Persians many lives, but had also provided the Greeks with a set of heroes to emulate.

Once they were through the pass at Thermopylae, Xerxes and the Persians moved quickly down the Attic Peninsula. They arrived at Athens in early September, but found the city largely deserted. Under the guidance of a magistrate named Themistocles, the Athenians had evacuated their city and moved by ship to the nearby island of Salamis.

Xerxes celebrated his triumph by burning large sections of Athens. The Acropolis was scarred, but not ruined. Xerxes then had his throne set up on a mountain so he could observe the upcoming fight between the Persian and Athenian fleets in the Bay of Salamis.

The Persians had a greater number of ships, and those ships were manned by the Phoenicians, considered the best sailors of the time. The Greeks had invested in their fleet, though, and the Greek trireme was both faster and more maneuverable than the Persian vessels.

The naval Battle of Salamis lasted an entire day. It was touch and go, with many moments when the battle looked bad for the Greeks. But by day's end, the Persian fleet retreated, having lost many sailors and ships. The Athenians were safe behind what the Oracle at Delphi had called the "wooden walls" of the trireme vessels.

Xerxes still controlled the Attic Peninsula, but he felt vulnerable having lost his fleet. Xerxes feared the Greek ships might go north and destroy his bridge of boats across the Hellespont. If they did so, he would be cut off from his source of supplies and reinforcements in Asia Minor. Therefore Xerxes made a fast retreat through Thessaly and Macedonia on his way home. He left a sizable Persian force in Greece, but it was wiped out at the Battle of Plataea the following year.

A group of small city-states had defied the power of the

Xerxes, the son of Darius the Great, planned an invasion of Greece to avenge the defeat of his father's army at Marathon. Despite a string of victories culminating in the burning of Athens, Xerxes could not complete his planned conquest and had to retreat.

greatest empire on earth. Greece was free, and she would continue to develop her unique brand of philosophy, art, poetry, and politics.

Xerxes was, in many ways, the last of the great Persian rulers. The Persian Empire continued long after his death, but it was no longer an expansionist realm. The quality of the leaders who followed showed a slow but steady decline, and by about 400 B.C., Greeks were intervening in Persian affairs, rather than the other way around.

Nearly 80 years passed before Greeks and Persians fought again. In 401 B.C., an Athenian soldier named Xenophon joined a group of Greek mercenaries who agreed to fight for Cyrus the Younger (not to be confused with his more illustrious ancestor, Cyrus the Great). The mercenaries went to Asia Minor and then to what is now Iraq where they fought a series of battles between Cyrus the Younger and his brother Artaxerxes II. Artaxerxes held the title of "King of Kings." Cyrus the Younger was trying to take that role and title from his brother.

Then, in the midst of the campaign, Cyrus was killed while leading a cavalry charge. The Greek mercenaries gathered to discuss the situation. Many were in favor of throwing themselves on the mercy of King Artaxerxes, since they were so far from home. But a core group, including Xenophon, argued in favor of making the long march home. As foreign adventurers, they could expect little mercy from the King of Kings. It was better to make the risky journey back to Greece.

What followed was an epic journey later described by Xenophon in his book, *The March of the Ten Thousand*. Xenophon and a handful of other courageous officers led the Greeks on a 1,300-mile journey of eight months' duration. They marched through areas few Greeks had seen and almost none had heard of until the publication of Xenophon's book. The climactic moment came when men shouted "The sea! The sea! The sea!" This was not the Aegean Sea, but the Black Sea, bordering on present-day Turkey. From there, Xenophon and his men were picked up by Greek trade ships. The long journey was over.

Years later Prince Alexander of Macedon would read Xenophon's book. Xenophon became Alexander's greatest Greek hero. The other great hero in Alexander's pantheon was Cyrus the Great who had united the Persians and the Medians.

As the spring of 334 B.C. approached, Alexander prepared to enter Asia. He would follow in the footsteps of Xenophon and seek to emulate Cyrus the Great in the creation of a worldwide empire.

FROM THE HELLESPONT TO ISSUS

Alexander crossed the Hellespont in the spring of 334 B.C. Known today as either the Hellespont or the Dardanelles, this narrow body of water separates Europe from Asia. The Hellespont leaves the Mediterranean Sea and flows into the Sea of Marmara, which then flows into the Bosporus. These three bodies of water—Hellespont, Bosporus, and Sea of Marmara—have been and remain the crossing points between Asia and Europe.

Alexander had with him about 35,000 infantry and 5,000 cavalry. It was a small force with which to invade the Persian Empire, but King Philip had trained these men well. They were disciplined, ferocious fighters whose admiration for their young king knew no bounds. They were ready to take on the greatest empire the world had yet known.

Alexander also had his closest friends with him. One was Hephastion, with whom he had studied in the school of Aristotle.

In 334 B.C., Alexander crossed the Dardanelles, otherwise known as the Hellespont, with a small army whose objective was to invade the Persian Empire. In his first battle with the Persians—and the first meeting between the Persians and the Greeks since the time of Xerxes—Alexander scored a victory at the Granicus River.

Another was Ptolemy, who was slightly older than Alexander and would become one of his confidantes. Still another was Parmenion, his father's most trusted general, who would serve as Alexander's second-in-command. Last and certainly not the least in importance was Bucephalus. The horse was older and slower now, but he remained Alexander's most treasured companion.

The Macedonian army came to the Hellespont. This was where Xerxes, the King of Kings, had created a bridge of boats in 480 B.C. Alexander had no such intention. His army was smaller and more mobile than the Persians had been. He wanted speed. The Macedonians crossed in a fleet of merchant ships hired for the occasion. Stories are told that Alexander sacrificed to the Greek god of the sea Poseidon as he crossed, and that as his ship neared the Asian shore he hurled a spear that stuck in the eastern bank—which seemed to declare that Asia would be his.

As soon as he had crossed the Hellespont, Alexander visited the ancient city of Troy, which had been the scene of a legendary ten-year siege, commemorated by the poet Homer in his epic song, the *Iliad*. Alexander knew the stories of the Trojan War by heart; in fact, he kept a copy of the *Iliad* under his pillow every night. Alexander and his closest friend Hephastion laid flowers at the graves of Achilles and Patroclus, both of whom had died in the great siege. By doing so, Alexander and Hephastion made a symbolic statement of their own close relationship. Whether they were lovers as well as friends is not known. Greek and Macedonian society alike encouraged close physical bonds between boys and young men. As he grew older, a man was expected to marry and raise children, but in his youth he was encouraged to be intimate with male friends, as a way of cultivating his maleness.

Leaving Troy (which later fell into ruin, and was rediscovered by the archeologist Heinrich Schlieman in 1870), Alexander and the Macedonians marched northeast. Less than 100 miles from the Hellespont, they met a Persian army which had gathered in response to Alexander's invasion.

The Persians and Greeks were close in number, each army having about 40,000 men. The Persians were commanded by the *satrap* (local ruler) who was responsible to the great King of Kings at the Persian capital. The Persians waited on the east bank of the Granicus River. If they could defeat him here, Alexander's invasion would come to a very abrupt end.

As he prepared for battle, Alexander knew and trusted in the quality of his men. The Macedonians fought in the phalanx formation. The phalanx, with its long spears and wall of shields, resembled a bristling porcupine or hedgehog. One of its great advantages was that the phalanx could move and turn to present its spears in any direction; therefore it could not be outflanked. Alexander also put his faith in the King's Companions, his group of elite cavalrymen. Raised on hardship and discipline, the King's Companions were intended to seize an opportune moment and shatter the enemy lines. Beyond their discipline and skill, the Macedonians had a great love for Alexander. They knew him since his boyhood, and they admired his stamina, courage, and daring.

The Persians who awaited the Macedonian attack also had a long and glorious military tradition. The Persian army, however, was composed of many subject nationalities, including Bactrians, Egyptians, and tribesmen from as far away as Afghanistan. The Persian army did not have the cohesiveness or the personal bonds that welded the Macedonians together.

There are those who also criticize the Persians for having grown soft. They had conquered the known world during the days of Cyrus and Darius, but they had grown accustomed to luxury. In the book of his campaign in Asia, Xenophon noted that the Persians of old had been accustomed to taking but one meal a day, but that the present Persians (of Xenophon's time) feasted all day long when they could.

The Battle of the Granicus River was the first major test of Greek and Persian strength since the days of Xenophon. Many accounts of the battle exist, but it is difficult to know which account to trust. It seems that Alexander made his attack straight across the river. The King's Companions encountered heavy resistance, and Alexander was slightly wounded in the head. But the Macedonian phalanx swept the Persians from their defensive position and put them on the run. It appears that the battle, though hard-fought, lasted only about two hours. Alexander had won his first conflict in Asia.

Rather than pursue the Persians, Alexander led his men on a back-and-forth march through Asia Minor (Turkey), capturing key strongholds of the enemy. One town that yielded to him without resistance was Gordium. Within the town there was an enormous knot of rope tied to an ox-wagon, known as the Gordian Knot (which even today is a metaphor for particularly difficult and seemingly unsolvable problems). Legend had it that the man who could untangle the knot would become the master of all Asia. Alexander naturally went to the site. He spent some time wrestling with the knot, to no avail. Then, looking at the task from a new angle, he pulled out his sword and clove the knot in half. The task was done; he was fated to become the Lord of Asia.

Some historians downplay the Gordian Knot; others make it into the greatest stroke of Alexander's life. What seems most important is that his men, who already thought him the greatest leader they had ever seen, knew about the legend and believed that this confirmed Alexander in his quest. They were now more ready to follow him than ever.

Alexander and his men subdued one stronghold after another. The port city of Halicarnassus put up an exceptionally stiff resistance, but Alexander's siege engineers found the remedy: they constructed wooden towers that brought their men closer to the walls. After Halicarnassus fell, Alexander marched into central Asia Minor and found his way into the mountain passes of what is now eastern Turkey. There he learned that the enemy had collected a new host.

Darius III, King of Kings, was the Persian ruler. Known for his beauty, charm, and wealth, Darius was not a warrior king. Yet Darius had no choice but to respond to this invasion. The Persian Empire was full of subject peoples, many of whom would revolt if they witnessed a successful invasion by an outside foe. Therefore Darius summoned a great army;

In the town of Gordium, Alexander came across an ox-cart tied with a rope whose knot had a legend ascribed to it—that anyone who could unravel it would become the master of all of Asia. After struggling with the knot, Alexander simply unsheathed his sword and cleaved the knot with it—another legendary moment in his extraordinary rise to power.

even the conservative estimates place it at around 200,000 men. He marched northwest from Babylon and reached the northeast corner of the Mediterranean before Alexander.

The Macedonians learned of Darius' approach. Alexander pushed his men at record speed in order to pass through the Cilician Gates before the enemy could block them. The gates, located in eastern Turkey, form a natural line of defense, where only four men can pass at any one time. This would have been the natural place to mount a defense, but Alexander's men passed them and reached the coastal plains of southeast Turkey.

When he learned of Alexander's march, Darius moved north by northeast. Without meaning to do so, the two armies bypassed one another completely. When Darius and Alexander each learned of one another's movements, they retraced their steps and met on the Plains of Issus. Because of their prior maneuvers, the Persians came from the north and the Macedonians from the south.

Issus is located very near the shore of the northeastern part of the Mediterranean Sea; today that water is called the Gulf of Iskenderum. Though he had the superiority of numbers, Darius paused and let Alexander make the first move. Darius' decision was a poor one, as Alexander could sense indecision and cowardice. Seeing that the Persians had chosen to meet him on the coastal plain, Alexander recognized that the narrow strip of land there favored his smaller, more compact army. The Persians would not be able to make use of their greater numbers. So Alexander planned his attack.

The Persians put their strongest units on their right, which was adjacent to the Mediterranean. Alexander kept just enough men on his left, facing the Persian right to contain this threat. The bulk of the Macedonians made a headlong attack on the Persian center. Alexander was in the thick of the battle.

The Persians did well on their right, pressing southward. The Macedonian phalanx continually moved northward, pressing in on the Persian center. Then, seeing his opportunity, Alexander launched a headlong charge with his Companions. The scene is well-known to millions of people today, because of Roman artwork that commemorated the moment. Alexander, riding Bucephalus, charged forward leading the Companions. Seeing this daring attack, Darius lost his nerve, turned, and fled. Dismayed by Darius' flight, the Persians began to give up in large numbers. Those on the Persian right flank fought stubbornly for some hours before they surrendered. By then, the day belonged to Alexander.

Darius fled the field, and galloped east as fast as he could. That night Alexander learned that the tent and belongings of the King of Kings had been found. Alexander and Hephastion went to see Darius' forsaken lodgings. There they found not only gold, silver, a bathtub, and other luxuries, but a small harem of women, including Darius' wife Stateira, her son, and Darius' mother Sisygambis.

All accounts agree that as Alexander entered the tent of Darius, Sisygambis stood up to greet the Macedonians. Mistaking Hephastion, Alexander's closest friend, for Alexander himself, the queen mother bowed deeply to Hephastion. Hephastion gestured to Alexander, and the queen mother realized her mistake. Anxiously she bowed again, this time to the true leader. Alexander stepped forward to reassure her of his good intentions. As for her mistake concerning his identity, he told her, "Never mind, mother. He is another Alexander."

It was a moment for the poets and the painters and sculptors to capture. It was full of romance and idealistic chivalry, but there is also a powerful piece of truth within the gesture: Alexander was indeed first among equals, a captain with many lieutenants. The Macedonian army would only follow him as long as the soldiers were confident he remained at the top of his form. In this rigorous form of leadership lay one of the keys to Alexander's success.

A somewhat humorous moment arose after Alexander came across Darius' mother, wife and others left behind after the Battle of Issus. Sisygambis, Darius' mother, accidentally bowed first to Hephastion, thinking he was Alexander. After Hephastion pointed out the Macedonian king, Alexander said good-naturedly, "Never mind, mother. He is another Alexander."

Although he had defeated her son and threatened to take away his empire, Sisygambis became devoted to Alexander, and he to her, treating her and the rest of Darius' family with respect and generosity.

A few days after the Battle of Issus, Alexander received a letter from Darius. The King of Kings lamented the fact that Alexander had invaded Persia and asked for the return of his family. In his reply, Alexander chastised Darius for the aggressions of his ancestors, Darius I and Xerxes. Alexander hinted that Darius might have had something to do with the murder of King Philip, Alexander's father. In conclusion, Alexander declared,

> Come to me, therefore, as you would come to the lord of the continent of Asia. Should you fear to suffer any indignity at my hands, then send some of your friends and I will give them the proper guarantees. Come, then, and ask me for your mother, your wife, and your children and anything else you please; for you shall have them, and whatever besides you can persuade me to give you.
>
> And in future let any communication you wish to make with me be addressed to the King of all Asia. Do not write to me as an equal. Everything you possess is now mine; so, if you should want anything, let me know in the proper terms, or I shall take steps to deal with you as a criminal. If, on the other hand, you wish to dispute your throne, stand and fight for it and do not run away. Wherever you may hide yourself, be sure I shall seek you out.

EGYPT'S
NEW GOD

Soon after his victory at Issus, Alexander made a leisurely journey down the eastern side of the Mediterranean Sea. It is surprising, given Alexander's impetuous nature, that he did not pursue Darius at once. But Alexander knew the importance of reducing the Persian fleet. As long as Persian ships were at his back, they could cut him off from communication with his homeland. Alexander did not have enough ships to fight the Persians at sea; therefore he decided to capture the coastal cities and thereby deny the Persians ports of entry.

Thus Alexander passed through Damascus on this way to the port cities of Byblus, Sidon, and Trye. The first two cities readily yielded; the inhabitants there had long resented Persian rule. From Byblus and Sidon, Alexander took ships that were the beginnings of his own fleet. Then he went a little further south and stopped at Tyre.

Alexander wanted to sacrifice to a god whom the Tyrians worshipped. This god resembled the Greek god Heracles (or Hercules).

The city of Tyre was legendary for being able to resist sieges throughout the ages. However, Alexander wanted it for strategic purposes and subjected it to a nine-month siege. After finally conquering Tyre, Alexander ended up crucifying the dead and selling the rest of the people into slavery.

Alexander, who claimed his inspiration from both Heracles and the hero Achilles, demanded to be allowed to sacrifice to the god within the city walls.

The Tyrians (people of Tyre) had a long and illustrious history. Tyre was a maritime city that sat on an island about a half-mile off the mainland. Its isolation from the land had rendered it almost impervious to land attack; Tyrians had withstood sieges even by the fearsome Assyrians 400 years earlier. Tyre was also the mother city of Carthage on the coast of North Africa. Counting on some help from their daughter city, the Tyrians resisted Alexander's demand for submission.

Alexander could certainly have bypassed Tyre on his way to Egypt. But to do so would leave the Persian fleet with a natural harbor from which to base its efforts. Therefore Alexander settled down to a siege of Tyre which required a type of effort quite different from the Battles of the Granicus or Issus.

The half-mile of water between Tyre and the mainland seemed an overwhelming obstacle, but Alexander directed his men in building a mole (causeway) out of earth, sticks, and stones. Tyre was separate from the mainland, but Alexander would bring the land to Tyre.

The first half of the mole was completed before the Tyrians sprang their surprise. As the water became deeper, the Tyrian ships were able to attack the mole from two sides, raining arrows and catapult shots on the Macedonian workers. Furious, Alexander had two great wooden towers built. His archers stayed in the towers and picked off the Tyrian sailors, while an immense net or shield between the two towers shielded the workers. All seemed well until the Tyrians made a surprise attack and burned both towers in one day.

Many leaders had besieged Tyre over the centuries. Most of them had given up by this point, but Alexander persevered. He left his men and the workers to continue while he went north to Sidon. There he recruited a fleet of almost 200 ships. When he sailed back to Tyre, he had a larger fleet than the Tyrians themselves. That, however, did not make them cower. The Tyrians built a causeway that divided their area into an inner and outer harbor. Alexander was welcome to the latter, but he could not penetrate the former.

Around this time, the Tyrians began to experiment with heated shot. They baked their projectiles before firing them. When these heated stones hit the Macedonian mole and ships, the ships were set on fire and men perished in horrible ways. Rather than let this be the final sign to abandon the siege, Alexander vowed vengeance.

Finally, after a siege of nine months, Alexander led his men in the final assault. Macedonian ships attacked from the outer harbor while Macedonian soldiers charged across the narrow mole. The fighting was fierce, but the Macedonians prevailed. By day's end, all resistance had ended and Alexander was master of the city which had defied him longer than any other place or foe.

Alexander took a thorough retribution. Some 2,000 Tyrians who had been killed were then crucified. The remainder of the population, about 30,000 in number, were sold into slavery. Tyre was rebuilt as a Macedonian city. Its status as the foremost Phoenician city was no more.

Geography too had changed. Tyre was an island when Alexander first saw it. When he left it had become a peninsula. As the years passed, sand and earth stuck in the wooden sections of the mole he had built. Today, 2,300 years later, Tyre is very much a peninsula, tied to the landmass of Lebanon.

All this begs the question: Was Alexander more or less ruthless than the average? Was his action at Tyre typical or more ferocious than average?

What seems to stand out is the length of resistance. Alexander was usually magnanimous toward fallen foes. But Tyre, like the Greek city of Thebes, had taken him off his own timetable. Therefore Alexander took a frightful vengeance on the people both of Thebes and Tyre. By the standards of his day, Alexander was one of the most vengeful of men. But if his record is applied against that of the Assyrians, 500 years earlier, or the Romans of 300 years later, Alexander appears "normal" by the standards of the ancient world. One thing he never did—and which the Romans later practiced—was to parade his victims in chains.

From Tyre, Alexander pressed south. He did not see

Some think that Alexander was uncharacteristically brutal towards the inhabitants of Tyre because of their long and costly defiance of his authority. Word of his conquest at Tyre spread rapidly, leading Persians in Egypt to surrender to Alexander at once without putting up a fight.

Jerusalem—one of the few great cities of the ancient world that he bypassed. Jewish oral history tells that Alexander came briefly to Jerusalem, and that he bowed down before the Chief Priest of the Temple, but this seems unlikely. It was not in Alexander's nature to bow before any man. Alexander took two months in another siege, this one of Gaza, and then moved across the Sinai Desert into Egypt.

The Persian commander and the garrisons in Egypt yielded at once. Alexander's reputation, and the knowledge of what he had done to the Tyrians, had preceded him. Alexander entered the capital city of Memphis, and his men enjoyed their first real rest in about two years.

Even Alexander and his tough, worldly men were awed by the spectacles of Egypt. The stonework, barges, canals, and palaces were far, far greater than anything Macedonia or even Greece had to offer. Though they may have previously heard of the Pyramids and the Sphinx, Alexander's men were cast into wonder by the actual sight of these architectural treasures. We now know that the largest of the Pyramids was built around 2600 B.C., making it more than 2,000 years old at the time Alexander saw it (knowledge of the Sphinx is less certain, but it is probably much older than the Pyramids).

Egypt had been under Persian rule for more than 150 years. The Egyptian upper-class welcomed Alexander as a liberator. He was enthroned as pharaoh and entrusted with the crook and flail, symbols of the royal authority. As Egypt's new pharaoh, Alexander was considered at least semi-divine. His men doubtless scoffed at the idea, but Alexander had been raised on the same idea by his mother Olympias. His time in Egypt appears to have reinforced the idea in his mind.

Soon after he was enthroned in Memphis, Alexander took part of his army on an exploratory expedition around the mouths of the Nile River. The Nile Delta, one of the largest in the world, evoked almost as much wonder as had the Pyramids. Alexander noted an important weakness in Egypt's development; despite her excellent internal communications via the Nile, she had little proper access to the Mediterranean world. Therefore Alexander sought a location for a new city. He found it in a large bay on the western end of the delta. There Alexander began to lay out plans for what would become Alexandria, one of the greatest cities of the ancient world. Alexandria became the capital city of General Ptolemy and his descendants. The

Ptolemies would rule Egypt from about 320 B.C. until the death of Cleopatra in 31 B.C.

When he finished laying out the boundaries of the new city, Alexander was seized by a desire to visit the oracle Ammon of Siwah, in the Libyan desert. Located about two hundred miles west of the Nile River, Siwah was a desolate location. There was no easy way to get there, but Alexander insisted. The words of his mother from many years earlier—that he was descended from the gods—pushed him forward.

The journey to the oasis at Siwah was one of the most punishing the Macedonians had yet endured. The heat was well over 110°F (43°C). The men pushed on, aided only by Alexander's intense desire. Arrian writes, "There is a commoner version of the story recorded by Aristobulus: according to this, Alexander's guides were two crows which flew along in front of the army; in any case I have no doubt whatever that he had divine assistance of some kind—for what could be more likely?"

When they arrived at Siwah, the Macedonians collapsed into a day or two of constant drinking and relaxation. Alexander went to the temple. All accounts agree that Alexander entered the temple and spoke at some length with the high priest of Ammon. When he came out, Alexander appeared chastened and somber. He gave no details then of what he had learned, but over the course of the next few years, word crept out that Alexander had received the following news—first, that he was the son of Ammon; second, that it was his destiny to rule all Asia; and third, that he must reach the farthest reaches of the Ocean Sea and sacrifice there to Ammon.

Even for a man who was accustomed to hearing his praises sung, this was extraordinary news. Alexander began to change after that day at Siwah. He became both more prideful and more daring. On the negative side, he became less inclined to listen to the words of others, even if the

While in Egypt, Alexander felt the need to visit the oracle Ammon of Siwah in the desert. Although the journey was hard and arduous—and, according to legend, guided merely by two ravens instead of any semblance of a map—Alexander got what he was looking for: confirmation that he was, in fact, descended from the gods.

words came from older and wiser men such as Parmenion.

Alexander and his men returned to Memphis. After a long rest and recuperation, the Macedonians left Egypt. They marched to Damascus in Syria and prepared for what they knew would be another struggle against Darius and the Persians.

ALL THE TREASURES OF THE EAST

Alexander headed east from Damascus. Darius headed west from Babylon. The two armies collided on an open plain called Gaugamela in what is now Iraq.

Darius arrived first and had time to prepare the ground. Knowing that Alexander could make use of almost any natural formation, Darius had his men sweep the field clear so that no vegetation or booby traps would impede the charges of his cavalry. Even the conservative estimates indicate that Darius had about 200,000 infantry and 40,000 horsemen. Some of these men had been recruited in faraway Bactria. They now converged on the open plain and awaited the Macedonian arrival.

Alexander appears to have enjoyed supreme self-confidence as the battle neared. His victories at Granicus, Issus, and Tyre had made his men believe that he was invincible. His encounter with the Egyptian priests at Siwah may have done the same for Alexander himself.

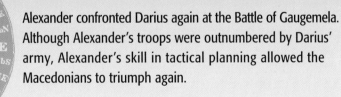

Alexander confronted Darius again at the Battle of Gaugemela. Although Alexander's troops were outnumbered by Darius' army, Alexander's skill in tactical planning allowed the Macedonians to triumph again.

Neither the great Persian numbers nor Darius' preparations appear to have caused Alexander any undue concern. He seems to have believed that it was his personal destiny to win and truly become the lord of all Asia.

The night prior to battle, Parmenion, one of Alexander's most trusted generals, urged him to make a night attack. There had been an eclipse of the moon just a few nights before, and Parmenion wanted to take advantage of the confusion that this might produce in the enemy (astronomers have dated the eclipse, allowing us to date the Battle of Gaugamela to October 1, 331 B.C.). Alexander refused Parmenion's proposal, stating that he would not steal a victory. So confident was Alexander that he slept soundly that night, and it took his courtiers to rouse him the next morning.

Stateira, the wife of Darius, died in Alexander's camp shortly before the battle. Alexander sent his condolences to Darius and then set about his preparations. It is not clear whether Stateira died of natural causes or whether her treatment at the hands of the Macedonians had been unchivalrous.

Knowing that he was outnumbered about five-to-one, Alexander refused to fight a conventional battle. As he gazed across the plain, Alexander clearly saw that the Persian army was made up of different national groups. There were Bactrians, Persians, Medians, Babylonians, and the like. It was an immense force, but the numbers and the different groups made for an unwieldy combination. Alexander made his plans accordingly.

As the battle began, Bucephalus was brought to Alexander. The trusty and beloved horse was seldom used these days in order to preserve him. But Alexander now mounted the companion of his boyhood. Horse and man now led the Macedonian army.

The Macedonian pike men, the men of the phalanx, lined up opposite the Persian center, where they could see the Indian elephants of Darius' army. But as the battle began, Alexander kept shifting his phalanx further to his own right. Reacting, Darius kept shifting his own infantry to his left to prevent Alexander from creating a flanking maneuver.

Darius launched his war chariots early in the battle. The ground had been smoothed and prepared for this action, but Alexander had found the remedy. As the chariots thundered forth, some of the most daring Macedonians ran out to meet them, thrusting their spears into the horse's bodies. The chariots soon dispersed, and Darius sent forth his elephants. These too failed to accomplish anything, as Alexander's men parted ranks and allowed the beasts to charge through without losses.

The Macedonian pike men engaged with Persian infantry. As was usually the case, the phalanx moved slowly forward, pushing its foes back. This caused disruption in the Persian lines which were already out of formation because of the shift to their own left flank. Suddenly a gap appeared in the Persian lines, and Alexander could make out the standard of Darius himself.

This was what Alexander had waited for. He gave the signal and led a headlong charge of the King's Companions straight at Darius. The Macedonians thundered across the plain, and, just as at Issus, Darius panicked. He turned his chariot and made his way to retreat.

The result was a disaster for the Persians. Even though some of their units had been fighting well and outflanked parts of the Macedonian army, the desertion of Darius was more than they could bear. Some Persian groups fought to the death, but most surrendered soon after the departure of their leader.

The King of Kings fled the field, escorted only by a handful of retainers. They galloped the 50 miles to their base camp at Arbela, pursued by Alexander and the Companions the entire way. Alexander and Bucephalus arrived at Arbela and found that the prey had escaped. In a sense, it did not matter. Nothing mattered any more in that Alexander had won the greatest battle of his career. There was no more resistance, and the way to the Persian heartland lay open.

Alexander moved slowly toward Babylon. This was a fabled city, first the capital of the Babylonian empire, and then one of the sub-capitals of Persia. The Babylonians opened their gates to Alexander as word of the Battle of Gaugamela had spread fast.

Alexander had achieved more than any Macedonian or Greek leader to this point. But he wanted more; he wanted to enter the great Persian capitals of Susa and Persepolis.

Susa has been described in the Bible's Old Testament in the Book of Esther. Esther describes Xerxes in the third year of his reign:

> He held high feast for all his lords and vassals; Persian warriors, Median notables, and the governor of every province . . . And when the festivity came to an end, he would entertain all the folk of Susa, high and low, for a whole week a banquet was spread for them at the gates of his garden, amid trees planted by art at the royal bidding.

There were, in truth, four Persian capitals: Susa, Persepolis, Parsagard, and Ecbatana.

Susa capitulated without a fight. The treasury found there contained at least 40,000 talents in silver. Alexander was suddenly the wealthiest man in the known world. He did not hoard the silver—saving or conservation were not among his skills. Having been raised in relative poverty by his tutors, Alexander was extremely generous in his bequests to friends, and silver was handed out at an alarming rate.

Then it was on to Persepolis, the ceremonial capital of Persia. The land changed as the Macedonians went east. Babylon and Susa were well-watered places, but as Alexander went further east he entered into what had been the heartland of Cyrus, a scorching hot area known as Parsa (today it is the Iranian province of Farshan).

Alexander first had to find a way through the Persian Gates,

After defeating Darius at Gaugamela, Alexander made his way to Babylon. After hearing word of Alexander's victory, the gates of Babylon were opened for Alexander's entrance rather than face a siege most likely ending in bloody defeat.

a narrow mountain pass that was as important to Persian defenses as the pass of Thermopylae was to Greece. A Persian force blocked the way, and many Macedonians died in a series of fruitless assaults. Then, just as had happened at Thermopylae, a traitor came forward. A Persian showed Alexander an alternative route. The Macedonians found there way through, and then made their way to Persepolis.

The grandeur of the palaces there defied description. Alexander and his men had already seen Egypt, but the Egyptian buildings were hundreds and thousands of years old, representing glories of an earlier age. Here at Persepolis, Alexander found monumental sculptures to the Persian Kings: Cyrus, Darius I, and Xerxes. There were monuments to the "Immortals," the 10,000-man bodyguard of the King of Kings. Yet all was empty and was Alexander's for the taking.

By now, Alexander had learned that Darius was at Ecbatana, hundreds of miles to the north. Since there was no threat from Darius, Alexander settled in for the winter at Persepolis.

Alexander paid a special visit to the tomb of Cyrus the Great at nearby Passeragarde. Cyrus had of course united the Persians and Medes around 550 B.C., and then had led them in the creation of the Persian Empire which Alexander now had conquered. The stone monument commemorating Cyrus has the following inscription:

> O, Man, whoever thou art, know that this is Cyrus who founded the Persian Empire and ruled the world. Grudge him not his monument.

Alexander paused a long time at the tomb. It was so simple, so unadorned, compared to the grand palaces at Persepolis, Susa, and elsewhere. Was this simplicity some type of ruse, or was it an even greater sign of Cyrus' magnificence? What type of monument might Alexander himself expect?

Sometime in the early spring of 330 B.C., the main palace at Persepolis burned. There were conflicting reports at the time, and historians have continued to debate the event to this day. Did Alexander set the fire? Was it through happenstance?

It seems likely that Alexander wanted to take some type of revenge for the Persian burning of Athens in 480 B.C. It is intriguing that he left Susa just as he found it, and that even Persepolis was not completely destroyed: outer buildings survived the fire. About all that can be said with certainty is that if Alexander meant to retaliate for the burning of Athens, he did so in a truly restrained manner since Persepolis had no civilian population to lose their homes.

TO THE ENDS
OF THE WORLD

E arly in the spring of 330 B.C., Alexander set out from Persepolis. He now had one simple goal: to find and capture Darius. Though he had been defeated in battle, lost his palaces and his treasury, the King of Kings remained an important symbol. Alexander's victory would not be complete until Darius was his. Alexander left 3,000 Macedonians under Parmenion to guard the palaces at Susa and Persepolis. The tiny size of this force indicates how thorough Alexander's conquest had been: resistance had evaporated in the face of his victories and his growing legend.

The chase led northeast from Persepolis. Alexander moved his men at a furious pace; to the north, Darius did the same with his men. As he pursued, Alexander had with him the ancient Artazabus, whom he had known 20 years earlier as a boy in Macedon.

Darius appears to have lost what was left of his political authority. His cousin Bessus, the satrap of Bactria, became the de facto leader

Alexander wanted to find and capture Darius in a symbolic gesture—the "King of Kings" serving under Alexander the Great. However, he was dismayed to find that Darius had been assassinated by one of his own men, Bessus.

of the group of Persian exiles. As they neared the shores of the Caspian Sea, Bessus stabbed and killed his cousin, then escaped. Alexander arrived just hours too late. He covered Darius' body with his own cloak and had the corpse sent to Persepolis for burial. The search was over. The King of Kings was dead.

Now, if ever, was the time for Alexander to turn for home. He had been away from Macedonia for four years, and he had accomplished far more than anyone might have expected. The former Persian Empire was now his. He could have arranged a dual sort of empire, with capitals both at Pella, Macedonia, and another at Susa or Persepolis. Certainly his faithful Macedonians believed the time had come to return.

Alexander never gave them the choice. He told his men that they must pursue Bessus, the escaped assassin. Otherwise,

Bessus would set himself up as a rival monarch in Bactria. If Alexander was to be the lord of all Asia, he must be done with Bessus and all other pretenders.

There was grumbling aplenty, but no sign of mutiny. The Macedonians wanted to go home, but they had long since learned to trust in the leadership of this boy who they had seen turn into a man. The pursuit of Bessus began.

Bactria had long been the eastern most part of the Persian Empire. If its extent were to be approximated today, Bactria would encompass all of what is today Afghanistan, a slice of what is now Pakistan, and the southern parts of the republics of Tajikistan and Uzbekistan. It was, therefore, an immense body of land and contained landscapes that varied from the mountains of the Hindu Kush to the plains of Central Asia. From here had come the cavalrymen who had been the best part of the Persian army, and from here tribute had flowed to Susa and Persepolis. Bessus reached Bactria long before Alexander and the his pursuit. Bessus was already the satrap of Bactria. Now, with Darius dead, Bessus proclaimed himself the King of Bactria.

Alexander's progress was delayed by two things. First, some tribesmen in the area just south of the Caspian Sea had made off with a number of the Macedonian horses—among them the old and treasured Bucephalus. Over the years they had been together, Bucephalus had probably saved Alexander's life half a dozen times. The horse was too old now to be ridden very much. He accompanied the army on its march, and Alexander rode him only on special occasions. Yet his importance to Alexander could not be underestimated. Alexander sent a warning that he would ravage the entire area and destroy every settlement unless his dearest companion was returned. According to Plutarch, the tribesmen brought Bucephalus and simultaneously rendered homage to Alexander. So relieved was Alexander that he gave them their freedom, and even paid them ransom money for Bucephalus.

The second factor that delayed the Macedonian march was unrest among some of his King's Companions. Soon after the death of Darius, Alexander began to wear Persian clothing. He had two or three new Persian advisers—foremost among them was Artazabus, who taught him about the traditions of court etiquette. Soon both Persians and Macedonians were expected to bow and scrape the ground on meeting Alexander. This type of behavior went completely against the Macedonian grain. The strength of the system that King Philip had built, and which Alexander had inherited, was the type of kinship and familiarity between the King and his Companions. Alexander's new conduct offended some of his oldest friends, and there were quiet stirrings of mutiny among the Macedonians.

Sometime that year, Alexander learned of a plot against his life. The plot was neither very sophisticated nor very advanced in its planning, but Alexander was shocked nevertheless. More than anything, he depended on the personal type of loyalty that he had enjoyed since his youth. To be threatened from within was something new and foreign to him. But worse news was yet to come. Alexander learned that Philotas, the commander of the King's Companions, had been informed of the plot and had neither informed Alexander nor acted to forestall the plan.

Philotas was one of the three sons of Parmenion; two others had already died in Alexander's service. It was unthinkable that such a man would not inform Alexander of any threat. With the evidence of Philotas' treason in his hands, Alexander acted as swiftly as he had against any of his other foes.

The camp was cordoned off; no one was allowed in or out. Philotas was brought to trial in the Macedonian style. Enraged over this treachery, Alexander acted as one of the prosecutors. Philotas was condemned and swiftly put to death.

At the same time, three of Alexander's couriers were speeding back to Ectabana, where Parmenion was in command of the Macedonian rear guard. Parmenion had not been implicated in the plot, but Alexander and all the Macedonians

Alexander chose to pursue Bessus over the rugged mountains of the Hindu Kush—a harsh route that pushed the army to the limits. Many suffered the effects from the cold, but Alexander encouraged his men along and somehow got his men to successfully complete their march in the spring of 328 B.C.

were well aware of the importance of "blood feud." This familial type of loyalty insisted that a man of honor avenge the deaths of his relatives. If Parmenion had not been a secret accomplice to the plot, he would nevertheless seek to avenge Philotas' death. The couriers went straight to Parmenion, who received them alone without bodyguards. Some records indicate that the couriers waited until Parmenion opened the two letters: one was from Alexander and the other was from Philotas. Seeing the letter from his son, Parmenion smiled. At that moment, the couriers became assassins. They struck down the 70-year-old Parmenion, wise and trusted general of first Philip II, and then his son Alexander.

What did the two letters contain? Was there a trap, laid by Alexander? Had Parmenion frowned, or had he been surprised at the letter from his son? Might the couriers have stayed their hands and knives? We do not know. Generally speaking, Alexander abhorred any kind of artifice or sneak attack. But he had been deeply shaken by the plot, and the hand of Philotas within that plot.

Alexander had acted with such speed and secrecy because he feared a rebellion from the troops of Parmenion. He now found other remedies. Those of Parmenion's soldiers who spoke against their King were grouped together in one new regiment and shown less favor. Alexander urged them to regain his trust by showing exceptional valor in the battles to come. Such were his means and his method, and such was his remarkable personality that most of the men were soon among his most loyal.

Finally, the time came to strike against Bessus. Knowing that Bessus had assembled great strength in numbers through-out Bactria, Alexander chose the hardest route by which to advance: over the mountains of the Hindu Kush into what is now Afghanistan.

The winter march was one of hardship and pain for all concerned. Crossing the mountain passes at about 11,000 feet, Alexander and his men suffered from cold, frostbite, and occasional cases of hypothermia. The animals suffered the worst; few of them survived to see the other side of the mountains. All writers agree that Alexander showed his sterling characteristics on the march. He was seen everywhere, encouraging, exhorting, pulling men out of snowdrifts, and forcing them on.

Sometime in the spring of 328 B.C., the Macedonians emerged on the eastern side of the Hindu Kush. Their march was one of the epochs of military history; chroniclers agree that it was more difficult than Hannibal's crossing of the Alps or Benedict Arnold's journey up the Kennebec River to attack Quebec in 1775.

Once on the other side, Alexander encountered little resistance. By now, his legend had grown so great that resourceful men such as Bessus virtually gave up when he appeared. Bessus was captured and executed in a most painful fashion. Alexander showed no respect for Bessus' body; he wanted to discourage the idea that Bessus had inherited the mantle of the King of Kings from Darius. Now it seemed that Alexander was truly without rivals. He was already the King of Kings, and he meant to finish the job by making his claim to be lord of all Asia.

India beckoned, but Alexander was not yet ready. Instead he embarked on a series of zig-zag marches through what is now Afghanistan and Uzbekistan. The Macedonians went all the way to the banks of the Oxus River, which Alexander decided would be the barrier between his empire and the world of the barbarians. In so doing, Alexander followed the lead of the Persians before him. Darius I, King of Kings, had been unable to subdue the Scythian tribes north of the Oxus. Alexander too left them alone.

Then it was southward through steppe, scrub brush, and over rugged mountain passes. No people in the world adore their homeland as much as the people of Afghanistan, but they recognize its thorny qualities. One Afghani legend declares that God made the world and found it good. Then he took up the rubble, sticks, and stones that were left over and put them in Afghanistan. Yet it was here, amid the rubble, that Alexander would find the first romantic love of his life: Roxanne.

Alexander's sexuality has been the subject of numerous studies. Modern gays and lesbians often claim Alexander as evidence that an alternative sexuality does not prevent a person from attaining spectacular success. The truth is, as usual, complicated.

Raised at the court of Macedon, Alexander was brought up in an intensely masculine world. That masculine influence was countered by the mystical beliefs of his mother, and she and Philip were virtually at war with one another throughout his youth. All this naturally led Alexander to suspect pair-bonding, whether it was between men and women, or men and men. There were, however, some important exceptions.

Hephastion, whom Alexander had praised to the Queen Mother of Persia, after the Battle of Issus, was probably Alexander's most intimate friend. Whether or not they were sexual lovers is not very important; they understood one another on a deep, soulful level.

Sometime after he arrived at the capital of Persepolis, Alexander was offered the gift of a Persian eunuch, known for his great beauty. The boy had been castrated at the court of Darius in order to preserve his physical features and voice. This boy became Alexander's lover, and the two seemed quite happy together (though many Macedonians were not happy, as they detested Alexander's Persian lover).

None of this was unusual for Alexander and the Macedonians. But his soldiers did expect that he would find female lovers as well. The first was the aforementioned Roxanne of Sogdiana.

As they traveled south from the Oxus River into Afghanistan, Alexander and his men noticed a princely stronghold at what was called the Rock of Sogdiana. Located several hundred feet above the mountain pass, the Rock appeared impregnable. Alexander nevertheless summoned its people to surrender. Apparently, the people there felt so secure in their moutainous position that they mockingly told Alexander to send up "winged soldiers" as they could be the only

After capturing the mountainous stronghold of Sogdiana, Alexander met and married the princess Roxanne—reportedly Alexander's first female lover, although his Persian eunuch and friend Hephastion were not discarded in lieu of his new wife.

ones who would be able to capture Sogdiana. Arrian writes of this event,

> He had called on them to discuss terms, and offered to allow them to return unmolested to their homes on condition of surrendering the stronghold; but their answer to the offer was a shout of laughter. Then in their barbaric lingo they told Alexander to ford soldiers with wings to capture the Rock for him, as no other sort of person could cause them the least anxiety.

Furious, Alexander called for volunteers to ascend the cliff that night. Dozens of men perished in the attempt, but a small number reached the top and presented themselves outside the gates in the morning. Astonished, the people of Sogdiana surrendered.

Within a matter of days, Alexander had met and married Roxanne, the prince's daughter. That she was exceptionally beautiful is beyond doubt, but she must have had even more— perhaps some type of inner strength and fearlessness that appealed to him. All we can say for sure is that Roxanne was the woman who Alexander loved the most. Even so, he did not discard either Hephastion or the Persian eunuch.

Two years after he had begun the pursuit of Bessus, and one year after he married Roxanne, Alexander altered direction. He and his faithful Macedonians headed south through the Khyber Pass, into India.

THE WATERS
OF INDIA

For the past three years, Alexander had fought peoples whom he considered "barbarians." Now he was filled with ambition to contend with other civilized peoples, among whom he considered to be those of Greater India.

"Civilized" and "barbarian" are of course relative words, as one person's culture may seem barbaric to another. What Alexander and most of the Macedonians believed was that in order to be civilized, people had to remain in one location for some time, build towns and cities, and develop some form of lasting government. Much of this definition came from Greece of the golden age of Athens, with the idea of the *polis,* or city-state, and its citizens.

Early in 326 B.C., Alexander entered what he called "India." Today it is the Republic of Pakistan, located just west of the Republic of India. Descending from the mountains, Alexander came upon a flat level plain that led right to the banks of the Indus River. Hephastion

The Indus was first seen by Alexander and his men in 326 B.C. It was a great river which exceeded both the Tigris and the Euphrates in waterflow, and the people had apparently settled near the Indus as early as 2500 B.C.

had gone ahead in advance and was already building a bridge of boats across the great river. Some day in May, Alexander and the army were ready to cross into the unknown.

The Macedonians realized that the Indus was one of the world's great waterways. It exceeded the Tigris and Euphrates in its flow, and its point of origin was as mysterious as that of the Nile (the source of the Nile was only found in 1872; the source of the Indus in 1907). The lands around the Indus were heavily populated by a people who claimed to have been there for millennia. Alexander may at first have doubted their claim, but modern archeology confirms that the banks of the Indus were settled as early as 2500 B.C.

There may have been some murmurs of discontent as the army crossed the Indus. The great river made a marking point that in some way seemed more ominous than the deserts, mountains, and steppe which they had crossed in Central Asia.

Of all the barriers that Alexander had previously encountered, only the Oxus River came close to the Indus.

Once across, the Macedonians marched through 60 miles of parched land to a greener, but very humid area known today as the Punjab ("Land of Five Rivers"). The Jhelum, Ravi, Beas, and Chenab all gather their waters together and then join the Indus in the southern Punjab. Alexander, though, was crossing the central Punjab; he did not know where the waters converged.

As he approached the Jhelum River, Alexander learned from his scouts that a large Indian army had gathered on the eastern bank. Led by King Porus of the Punjab, the Indian army had numbers about as large as Alexander, and a number of elephants as well. Men atop the elephants were ready to pour out a hailstorm of arrows on any opponent. Perhaps it was here that Alexander realized fighting a "civilized" opponent might be more hazardous than taking on "barbarian" peoples.

The Battle of the Jhelum raged all day long. Alexander got most of his army across the river early on in the battle, but the Indians fought more tenaciously than any opponent he had seen since the siege of Tyre, eight long years ago. Though they took far greater losses than the Macedonians, the Indians fought relentlessly, and their elephants managed to stampede many of the Macedonian horses. Only late in the day did Alexander triumph. The Indians pulled back, leaving their king to be captured. Porus, bleeding from many wounds, was brought before Alexander who asked the captured monarch how he wished to be treated.

"Like a king!" replied Porus.

We do not know whether Porus had heard tales of Alexander previous to the battle. We can say, for certain, that Porus' response was the perfect one: the type that Alexander was bound to admire and respect. Within a matter of days, Porus had become a friend and ally of Alexander.

It was fortunate for Alexander that he had found a new

friend because one of his oldest and closest had just died. Sometime after the Battle of the Jhelum River, old Bucephalus breathed his last.

Bucephalus was then almost 30 years old. He had not been used in battle since the climactic Battle of Gaugamela. Rather he had been treasured as Alexander's boon companion, and perhaps as a good luck charm. Alexander was deeply moved by the death of his lifelong friend. He ordered that two new cities be built, one on either side of the Jhelum River. The city on the west bank was to be called "Victory" and the east bank city was named after Bucephalus. Today, numerous towns and villages on the Jheulm River claim to be the resting place of Bucephalus, who is perhaps the most honored horse of all human history.

Then it was on, to the east. With Porus to provide information about his foes, Alexander felt ready to conquer all India. It appears that the Egyptian priests at the Temple of Siwah had told Alexander he must give offering to Zeus at the farthest reaches of India. By doing so, he would fulfill his destiny.

Unfortunately, that destiny was about to be thwarted. As they neared the banks of the Rav, another one of the five rivers that make up the Punjab, Alexander's men grumbled, complained, and finally asked to speak to their commander.

Alexander met the leaders of his men. He was confident he could win them over; after all, he had always done so, for years upon years.

Alexander gave one of his most stirring speeches. He reminded the men of all the armies, peoples, and geographic obstacles which they had conquered in the past. He made an interesting comparison to Heracles, saying that if the Greek hero had stopped at the second or the fifth of his twelve great labors, that history would not honor his name so profoundly. Let the troops follow; Alexander would lead them to yet greater glories.

There was silence. As bewildered as he had ever been, Alexander urged someone to speak. The one who stepped

The defeated Indian king Porus was brought before Alexander. When Alexander asked Porus how he should be treated, Porus replied "Like a king!" This answer greatly pleased Alexander, and the two became friends.

forward was Coenus, who had been a faithful and enterprising leader all the way from Macedonia to this point. He said to Alexander,

> Sir, we appreciate the fact that you do not demand from us unreasoning obedience. You have made it clear to us that you will lead us on only after winning our consent, and, failing that, that you will not use compulsion. This being so, I do not propose to speak on behalf of the officers here assembled, as we, by virtue of our rank and authority, have already received the rewards of our services and are naturally concerned more than the men are to further your interests. I shall speak, therefore, for the common soldiers . . .

Every man of them longs to see his parents again, if they yet survive, or his wife, or his children; all are yearning for the familiar earth of home, hoping, pardonably enough, to live to revisit it, no longer in poverty and obscurity, but famous and enriched by the treasure you have enabled them to win. Do not try to lead men who are unwilling to follow you; if their heart is not in it, you will never find the old spirit or the old courage. Consent rather yourself to return to your mother and your home. Once there, you may bring good government to Greece and enter your ancestral house with all the glory of the many great victories won in this campaign . . . Sir, if there is one thing above all others a successful man should know, it is when to stop. Assuredly for a commander like yourself, with any army like ours, there is nothing to fear from any enemy; but luck, remember, is an unpredictable thing, and against what it may bring no man had any defense.

Coenus' speech was followed by loud applause. He had dared to speak what all others had thought, but had been too afraid to say. The fear had been with good reason, because Alexander was furious. He cried that there were men who would follow him willingly, and that he released all others to go their own way. Then Alexander, like his hero Achilles from the Trojan War, retired and sulked in his tent. He remained there three days, hoping the men would change their mind. But for once, Alexander had encountered a force he could not overcome: the desire of his men to see Macedonia once more.

Three days later, Alexander had his soothsayers take the omens. The priests returned with the word that the omens were unfavorable. Alexander then relented and magnanimously agreed that the army would return home. The shouts of joy were thunderous. Alexander, the men said, had conquered everyone and everything, but he had yielded to their will. Little did they know what he had in store for them.

PERILOUS JOURNEYS

The Jhelum was the farthest east Alexander would go. He did not allow his men to lead him by the nose or to return by the route they had come. Instead, Alexander announced that he must see the Great Ocean; therefore, the Macedonians began to built boats and ships to carry them down the Indus River.

The Indus today is a rather small river below the famed Tarbela Dam of northern Pakistan. This was not the case in Alexander's time. He had his men had to make every provision against storms, flash floods, and even the possibility of a monsoon coming inland.

The people of India (what is now Pakistan) were not docile either. Perhaps because their Brahmin priests fortified them with words of encouragement, the Indians fought Alexander more fiercely than any other civilian population he had encountered. Just reaching the junction of the Chenab and Indus rivers took two city sieges. Both cities were stormed and many of the inhabitants were slain. Alexander's

After an assault on a city in what is now Pakistan, Alexander was feared dead after he and only three other soldiers had begun fighting enemy forces. Although he was actually still alive, the wounds Alexander suffered would plague him the rest of his life.

men, worn out from years of campaigns and months of India's difficult climate, were near their breaking point.

So, for that matter, was Alexander. He showed little interest in his wife Roxanne or in cultivating the rich friendships that had always been so important in his life. In the autumn of 326 B.C., Alexander seemed older than his thirty years. Older, more weary, but not more patient or forgiving.

As they made a frontal assault on a city in the Sindh area of what is now Pakistan, Alexander became frustrated by his men's lack of vigor. Seizing a siege ladder, he charged up the ramparts of the city and found himself at the top of the battlements with only three companions. His foes, recognizing him as the Macedonian leader, began to hurl missiles and fire arrows at him. The situation was desperate.

Rather than try to go back down the ladder, Alexander leapt from the battlements into the foreign city. His three companions followed his example, and soon the Macedonian king and three others were fighting dozens, if not hundreds of their foes.

Among the Macedonians outside the city, word spread that Alexander had been killed. Filled with the fire of anger and desperation, the Macedonians both scaled the ladders and managed to break through a gate. They entered the city and found their king prostrate on the ground. It was a frightening moment. Among other problems, Alexander had never designated a successor. The Macedonians fought on and within two hours had subdued the entire city. Many civilians were massacred by the Macedonians, who had not yet learned that Alexander was still alive.

Alexander had been taken away on a stretcher. Though he had not been trampled or lost any of his limbs, an enemy ax had entered his chest and punctured his lung. Most men would have died that afternoon, but Alexander's remarkable constitution saved him.

It was four days before Alexander appeared in front of his men once more. Though he shouted and waved as boldly as ever, he was not the same man. He never would be the same; this wound had been too deep. The ax had been removed by a surgeon, but air had escaped Alexander's lungs in the process. The healing was incredibly slow, and there would be no relief for the pain that followed. Such a severe wound in such a tender area leaves a mass of scar tissue; the result was that every time he breathed heavily or spoke loudly, Alexander experienced a fierce pain in his side. He became adept at concealing the depth of his injury, but he was a man in pain for the rest of his life.

The army continued down the Indus River. When they reached the immense Indus Delta, Alexander took a select handful of men out to the ocean. They landed on an island about 20 miles out, where Alexander made sacrifices to Poseidon and Zeus. Though he had not reached the farthest extent of

Alexander led his men through the Makran Desert, or the Desert of Gedrosia as it is also known. The environment proved to be too much for many of his men and horses, and water—as well as high morale—was scarce.

India, he had reached the southern ocean.

Returning to the main body of men, Alexander announced his plan to split the force in two. Half would explore the coast of what is now Pakistan and Iran while the other half would march overland with Alexander. Knowing that previous leaders such as Cyrus the Great and Semiramas had come to grief in the desert, Alexander promised to do his utmost for all concerned. The land army would occasionally go to the coast and set up supplies of food and water for the men of the fleet, which would be commanded by Nearchus, one of Alexander's boyhood friends.

It took some weeks to put everything in order, but Alexander's commands were followed. The two forces took their leave of one another; for many of the veterans, it was the first separation from their fellows in nine years of service.

Alexander and the land army marched north along the Indus, then struck west into the area known either as the Makran or the Desert of Gedrosia. Even though Alexander had heard tales of Cyrus' march, he must not have known what he was taking his men into. It is inconceivable that he, with the careful care he had shown over the years, would expose them heedlessly to such danger.

Even today in the early 21st century, outsiders do not often travel in what is now the province of Baluchistan. The Baluchii tribesmen are hospitable, but the environment is harsh. Most of the time, Baluchistan endures intense heat that creates mirages in the desert; then, for brief periods, intense rainfall occurs which creates flash floods that can carry away all-terrain vehicles.

It was much worse for Alexander and the army. Most of the horses died within the first two weeks. Those that survived had to be nursed along. Water ran out a number of times, and when water was available, it was rationed. Once, the army made its way to the coast and set up caches of food and supplies for the fleet, but that short trip to the ocean only convinced the men that they had been brought into the reaches of Hell. Few places on Earth are more barren than the Makran coast; the landscape sometimes resembles the craters of the moon.

Three weeks into the desert, Alexander knew the decision had been a terrible mistake and his single greatest miscalculation. To attempt to return would make morale worse, and when they returned to the Indus Delta, his famished and footsore men would be easy prey for any Indian lord who decided to attack them. It could only be forward.

To set a proper example, Alexander dismounted, and walked the rest of the way. Usually he was at the head of the column. Given his grevious wounds from a few months before, and the pain that scar tissue can cause, one can only guess that he was in quiet anguish nearly the entire time. Yet he gave little sign; to the men he was Alexander, King of Macedon, Lord of Asia, the greatest man of their era.

One of the most touching narratives of this desperate time period comes from the chronicler Arrian who relates what happened when Alexander was offered a drink. Arrian wrote,

> Alexander, with a word of thanks for the gift, took the helmet and, in full view of the troops, poured the water on the ground. So extraordinary was the effect of this action that the water wasted by Alexander was as good as a drink for every man in the army.

The scene has been commemorated in art. The moment was probably one of Alexander's finest. It shows him to have been a master of theater, even when the roof was crashing in around him.

If anything, the journey became even more hazardous. The Macedonians staggered on, led by their indomitable commander. Most of the soldiers had little idea of the pain Alexander suffered. The wound in his chest must have given him moderate pain every time he breathed heavily, yet he continued on. So did his men.

Finally, after 60 days in the desert, Alexander and his men reached a rendezvous point near the Straits of Hormuz (this area is known today as the most congested spot for oil tankers anywhere around the globe). At the time, the area was quite undeveloped, but there was water aplenty. The exhausted, parched, and weary men sank down and drank their fill.

Alexander allowed his men a full seven days of parties, full of food and wine, to celebrate their miraculous survival. Feasts were held in the honor of the god Dionysus, and the

Finally, upon reaching the Straits of Hormuz, Alexander and his men stopped to rest and recover from their desert ordeal. Here he also joined up with Nearchus whom he had sent to explore the coast of what is now Pakistan and Iran.

Macedonians, who had always been hard drinkers, turned into compulsive alcoholics (as we might label them today)—and Alexander was one with his men. The pain from his wound and the emotional exhaustion caused by the strain of leading his men through the desert had impaired both his judgment and his spirit. He would not be the same again.

One of the few bright spots of this time came when Alexander met Nearchus and a handful of followers near the Straits of Hormuz. Nearchus looked every bit as bad as Alexander had when he first arrived, and the tiny number of companions gave Alexander great alarm. Was this, he asked, all that remained of the men who had boarded the fleet?

No, not at all, the answer came. Though they had endured serious hardships, the men of the fleet had come through with very few losses. The ships too, were safe and sound.

This was at least something to be thankful for. Alexander never wearied of hearing Nearchus' tales of the fleet and its voyage. The stories Nearchus told were much more appealing than the recounting of the dreadful journey by land.

Alexander, Nearchus, and the reunited army moved by slow stages to Persepolis and then to Susa. They had returned to central Persia, which, many of them began to realize, was Alexander's new home. Whether it would be theirs as well was still open to question.

10

THE PRICE OF GREATNESS

In the last year that remained to him, Alexander displayed some of his best qualities, as well as some of his most repulsive ones. Though he acted as if he were just beginning in life, even Alexander must have known that his days were short. The constant pain in his chest and side, coupled with the heavy bouts of drinking, reduced him at times to a shadow of his former self.

Soon after he returned to Persepolis, Alexander learned that the tomb of Cyrus the Great, located at Passergarde, had been plundered. Alexander went straight to the tomb, which still stands in the desert of Iran. Alexander ordered that the tomb be restored and that the inscription be written a second time, now in Greek. It reads:

"O man, I am Cyrus, son of Cambyses, who founded the empire of Persia and ruled over Asia. Do not grudge me my monument."

This scene depicts Alexander's marriage to Barsine, the eldest daughter of Darius, at the palace of Susa. This wedding ceremony also married 80 Macedonian officers with Persian women, including Hephastion, who married a younger sister of Barsine. According to the historian Arrian, the wedding was conducted under Persian traditions.

It is a simple inscription for such a great man. Alexander stood a long time before the tomb in silence. Perhaps he sensed the fleeting nature of power and glory.

Alexander could always rouse himself to perform a theatrical show. One of the most significant was the great joint wedding at Susa.

Soon after his return from the Gedrosian Desert, Alexander announced his intention to marry Barsine, the eldest daughter of Darius, the former King of Kings. Hephastion, who remained Alexander's most constant friend, would marry a younger sister of Barsine. About 80 other Macedonians officers would marry Persian women of noble blood. The ceremonies were conducted in the palace at Susa, and the wedding owed far more to Persian tradition than Macedonian.

According to Arrian:

> The marriage ceremonies were in the Persian fashion: chairs were set for the bridegrooms in order of precedence, and when heaths had been drunk the brides entered and sat down by their bridegrooms, who took them by the hand and kissed them. The King, who was married just as the others were, and in the same place, was the first to perform the ceremony—Alexander was always capable of putting himself on a footing of equality and comradeship with his subordinates, and everyone felt that this act of his was the best proof of his ability to do so. After the ceremony all the men took their wives home, and for every one of them Alexander provided a dowry. There proved to be over 10,000 other Macedonians who had married Asian women. Alexander had them all registered, and every man of them received a wedding gift.

This, however, was one of the last times that Alexander would experience harmony with his own men. Strains had built between him and them—strains that were soon to burst open.

Many Macedonians now believed that Alexander had gone too far. He no longer seemed like their fearless leader, under whom they had conquered the Persian Empire. Rather, he seemed more like a Persian than a Macedonian. In spite of his agreement to turn home when they reached the Beas River in India, Alexander showed no sign whatever of heading to Macedonia. Susa, Perspeolis, and Babylon were now more important to him than Pella, Athens, or the mountains of Thessaly.

There were rumors, too, that Hephastion had become more than Alexander's best friend. With no designated successor, Alexander leaned more heavily than ever upon Hephastion's judgment. Accounts vary as to whether Hephastion merited this trust. Some chroniclers assert that Hephastion remained loyal and virtuous to the end, but others hint at corruption and the selling of offices.

In either event, it was clear that no one could reach Alexander without the good will and permission of Hephastion and a handful of brother officers. Alexander was now almost cordoned off from his veterans, the men who had made possible all his great conquests. Resentment came to a peak when Alexander held a mass gathering of 10,000 Macedonians. Their services, he announced, were no longer required. They were free to go home.

Considering their near-mutiny on the Beas River in India, one would expect the soldiers to jump at the chance to leave. Instead, voices were raised. Accusations were made that Alexander had betrayed his own people and become a Persian. As the mood turned ugly, some of the troops even shouted, "You go home. Go walk in the desert with your Father!"

This obvious reference to the god Ammon prompted Alexander into a rage. Rather than withdraw, he leapt off the platform right into the crowd of disaffected soldiers. Using his fists, he attacked the loudest of the rebellious men. This brought many of the men to tears. Soon they were falling on their knees, begging his forgiveness. Alexander pardoned them, and allowed the men to chose whether to go home to Macedonia or to remain in Persia.

It was one of the great scenes of a life that was full of drama. It was also one of the last. Despite his untamed vigor and courage, Alexander was sinking under the weight of his wounds and the alcohol he consumed each night. He rose later and later, and sometimes he was only functional for about three hours of daylight.

Even the greatest of men are susceptible to illness and disease. Alexander had spent his life defying the odds. Now the more common varieties of frailty had caught up with him.

Friendship had always been one of the cornerstones of Alexander's life. Without friendship he would not have survived his early years, witnessing the intense conflicts between Philip and Olympias. Now the most central part of the cornerstone fell away when Hephastion died.

Hephastion had been in good heath, and his sudden demise naturally raises suspicion. Might he have been poisoned? Historians have never proven foul play in Hephastion's demise, but suspicions remain. For one thing, Cassander, the son of Antipater, the regent of Macedonia, had recently arrived at Alexander's court. Cassander had been bitter rivals with both Alexander and Hephastion in their youth. Now, Cassander was his father's representative, asking Alexander for help in the ongoing power struggle between Antipater and Olympias. At the time, however, Alexander spent no time on such thoughts because he was consumed with grief. Perhaps the built-up grief of comrades lost had silently added up, but Alexander virtually collapsed for about a week. For two days he could not be removed from the corpse, and even after that he appeared haggard and weary. Alexander planned a magnificent funeral pyre for Hephastion's corpse, then turned to the business at hand.

Alexander was cool, even cold toward Cassander, but he does not seem to have transferred his antipathy toward the father. Antipater was confirmed in his position as regent, and Alexander sent letters to his mother, asking her to cause less trouble with Antipater. "Asking" is a word we seldom use with Alexander, but in his relations with Olympias, he usually was a model of decorum and politeness.

Alexander and the army left Ecbatana for Babylon. As they neared the city, a group of priests came forward and asked the king not to enter Babylon. The omens were bad, they said, and it would be better for the king to spend some time waiting outside.

Alexander deferred and made camp to the west of Babylon. Whether he actually believed the omens or not, this was a surprising development. The Alexander of a decade ago, or even three years ago, would have brushed past the omens and insisted on entering his capital.

The army entered the city a few weeks later. Soon it became apparent that Alexander was seriously ill. It came on as a fever in mid-May and steadily worsened. By the beginning of June, Alexander was confined to his bed. He held one last review of his troops. Soldiers slowly filed through the royal suite, and Alexander, who could barely speak, managed to acknowledge hundreds of men by nodding his head or moving his eyebrows. The entire scene was one of tragedy and doom.

Sometime on the day of his death, Alexander was asked about who would succeed him. All accounts agree that Alexander managed to gasp out, "To the strongest." There is some discrepancy in the translation with some scholars believing that the words he used meant "To the best."

Alexander died on the tenth of June in the year 323 B.C. He was about a month shy of his 33rd birthday. Legend has it that Sisygambis—Darius' mother, whom Alexander had taken after the Battle of Issus—turned to a wall and fasted until she died, grief-stricken upon hearing of Alexander's death. When the news reached Athens, someone said, "Alexander dead? Impossible! The world would reek of his corpse."

Conqueror of numerous lands and numerous peoples, but mortal after all, Alexander was gone to the world.

Years later, the historian Diodorus published a series of plans that he claimed Alexander had formed within a few months of his death. If they were authentic, the plans indicate that Alexander was not satisfied and felt that he had new lands to conquer.

First, the plans envisioned a rapid conquest of the northern Arabian Desert. Then, the subject peoples along the eastern rim of the Mediterranean Sea were to build 1,000 warships, aboard which Alexander and his men would sail to defeat Carthage. The daughter city of Tyre located in what is now Tunisia, Carthage was the strongest maritime power of the western Mediterranean. By defeating Carthage, Alexander would open the way for a road that would be paved to the Pillars of Heracles (today known as the Straits of Gibraltar). From there, there were other plans intending to take Macedonian rule all the way to Britain.

Given Alexander's physical condition and the despondency he had shown after Hephastion's death, the plans seem absurdly ambitious. How could a king conquer the rest of the Mediterranean and most of northern Europe when he staggered from one drunken episode to another? Yet here is part of the riddle of Alexander. Knowing his own weakness and knowing the challenges that lay ahead, he still seems to have planned great things.

The feud over the succession began almost at once. Lacking clear instructions from the departed Alexander, many men and some women thought they should be the ones to rule in Alexander's place. Roxanne, who had been spurned in favor of Barsine, now murdered both Barsine and Alexander's infant son. Back in Macedonia, Olympias continued to feud with Antipater. Olympias outlasted Antipater, but fell victim to his son. Cassander had her tried and sentenced to death in 314 B.C. Cassander later had Roxanne and her son murdered. By about 305 B.C., Cassander was the clear king of Macedonia, without any interference from the previous royal family. Cassander ruled Macedonia until his death in 297 B.C.

Not even Alexander's corpse was immune from the rivalries between his former generals. Many of Alexander's followers believed his body should be brought back to Macedonia. But a minority opinion prevailed that the body should go to the Temple of Ammon at Siwah.

A magnificent funeral procession wound its way from Babylon to Egypt. There the corpse was intercepted by Ptolemy, one of Alexander's generals. Believing that the Egyptians would honor Alexander, and by extension himself, Ptolemy stopped the funeral car and had it brought to the new city of Alexandria.

In the years that followed, Ptolemy became the new ruler of Egypt. Others of Alexander's generals carved out kingdoms for themselves in Asia Minor and the Middle East. Some of Alexander's officers even started small kingdoms in what are now Afghanistan and Uzbekistan.

Now it has been approximately 2,300 years since Alexander died. Can we measure his place in history?

As a man, he must rank among the very top in charisma.

The noble funeral procession of Alexander the Great went from Babylon to Egypt, where Ptolemy, one of Alexander's generals, took his body for himself and laid Alexander to rest in Alexandria. This set the stage for Ptolemy to become ruler of Egypt, as many of Alexander's officers would go on to rule various regions of the mighty empire.

Very few people in human history have convinced large groups of men—such as the Macedonian army—to travel such distances, fight such battles, and endure such perils. To use a 20th-century analogy in the D-Day campaign, neither Dwight Eisenhower nor Bernard Montgomery landed with their men on the beaches of Normandy. Warfare has changed, to be sure. Commanders today spend their time in bunkers and situation rooms in order to coordinate movements. However, we still have the right to ask: Could Eisenhower, Montgomery, or even the formidable George Patton have convinced men to travel thousands of miles on foot—through countries for which they did not even have maps? Using the World War II analogy, the best that can be said is that Alexander combined some of the finest qualities of both George Patton (headstrong attack) and those of Erwin Rommel (chivalry, courage, leadership by example).

In his ability to inspire and motivate men, Alexander stands among the top five military commanders on virtually any list. As a battlefield commander, the surest proof of his greatness is that Alexander never lost a battle. He won through decision, speed, brilliance, and the force of his personal example. In this realm, Alexander stands among the top ranks of all time. Only Julius Caesar, Napoleon, and Genghis Khan are in his peer group.

As a conqueror, Alexander has a mixed record. There are numerous examples of his chivalry and compassion toward the defeated (such as toward the family of Darius after the Battle of Issus), but there are also scenes of his vengeance, such as after the taking of Thebes and of Tyre. There are groups of people in Persia (today Iraq and Iran) who remember him as "Alexander the Barbarian," or "Alexander the Horned One." One of the worst stories of Alexander comes from his time in Bactria. Alexander came across a group of Greek-speaking people, who had been conquered by the Persians a century and a half earlier and brought from Asia Minor to Bactria. Learning that they were descendants of the men who had guarded the oracle of Dyamis, Alexander slaughtered the Greeks in Bactria.

Finally, how did Alexander affect the course of history?

Some scholars, who want to devalue the importance of military history, might say that Alexander was a military man, pure and simple, and that he did not change the world. To that, one can only say that few other military men, and few men from any occupation or walk of life, have changed the world as much as did this Macedonian in 33 years.

When Alexander was born, Persia was the greatest empire in the western world. When he died, he had created the makings of a new Macedonian empire, but it fractured into four or five separate parts. When Alexander was born, Greek culture was limited to Greece, its northern territories, and the islands of Crete and Cyprus. When Alexander died, Greek culture had made inroads as far east as the Indus River valley. Within 100 years of his death, Greek language, literature, poetry, and arts would be taught in hundreds of cities throughout the western world.

The Athenian had been right. Alexander was dead, and the world did reek of his corpse. Alexander's effect was seen from Macedonia to India and from the Oxus River to the Nile.

The ruins of numerous city-states throughout the Middle East testify to his introduction of Greek culture. Horsemen in Pakistan and Afghanistan still claim that their horses are descendants of Bucephalus. Legends abound of "Alexander slept here," and "Alexander passed this way." One of the very best legacies, however, is preserved among the Greek sailors and fishermen of the Aegean Sea. Even today, it is claimed, fishermen must be ready to answer the mermaid's question.

A fishing boat is tossed about by sudden waves. A mermaid appears and demands, "Where is my brother, Great Alexander?"

All Greek fishermen know they must deliver the right answer. The wrong answer will provoke the mermaid to wrath, and she may well sink their boat. The one, and only, correct answer, is:

"Great Alexander lives. And still rules!"

356 B.C.	Alexander, first child of Philip and Olympias, is born.
354	Cleopatra, second child of Philip and Olympias, is born.
344	Aristotle arrives at Pella and becomes a tutor to a select group of youths, among them Alexander.
340	Alexander becomes regent in his father's absence.
338	Philip and Alexander lead the Macedonian army to a stunning victory over Thebes at Chareonea.
336	Philip is assassinated by a courtier. Alexander becomes king.
335	Alexander captures Thebes and destroys the city.
334	Alexander and about 35,000 Macedonians cross the Hellespont and invade Asia Minor, part of the Persian Empire.
333	Alexander defeats Darius at the Battle of Issus.
332	Alexander besieges and takes the city of Tyre.
332	Alexander enters Egypt.
332	Alexander visits the Temple of Ammon at Siwah.
331	Alexander defeats Darius at the Battle of Arbela (also known as Gaugamela).
330	Alexander burns Persepolis.
330	Darius dies by the hand of his cousin Bessus.
329	Alexander pursues Bessus into Bactria.
328	Alexander captures Bessus. Alexander reaches the Oxus River, a natural division between the former Persian Empire and the land of the Scythians.
327	Alexander marries Roxanne, a Sogdian princess.
326	Alexander crosses the Indus River. Battle of the Jhelum River takes place.
325	Alexander and half his army cross the Gedrosian Desert.
324	Alexander and 80 of his men take Persian brides.

323 Alexander dies in Babylon.

319 Antipater dies in Macedonia. The fragile alliances that had continued between Alexander's generals disintegrate.

314 Cassander, son of Antipater, becomes the King of Macedonia. He had Olympias killed.

309 Cassander has Roxanne and her son murdered.

305 Cassander rules in Macedonia till his death in 297 B.C.

Barnes, Jonathan, editor. *The Complete Works of Aristotle*. Princeton: Princeton University Press, 1984.

Crompton, Samuel Willard. *100 Military Leaders Who Shaped World History*. San Francisco: Bluewood Books, 1999.

Crompton, Samuel Willard. *100 Battles that Shaped World History*. San Francisco: Bluewood Books, 1997.

Fox, Robin Lane. *The Search of Alexander*. Boston: Little, Brown & Company, 1980.

Godolphin, Francis R.B., editor. *The Greek Historians: The Complete and Unabridged Historical Works of Herodotus, Thucydides, Xenophon, Arrian*. New York: Random House, 1942.

Herodotus, *The Histories*. Aubrey de Selincourt and John Marincol, eds. London: Penguin Books, 1954.

Hicks, Jim and the Editors of Time-Life Books. *The Persians*. New York: Time-Life Books, 1975.

Hornblower, Simon and Tony Spawforth. *Who's Who in the Classical World*. Oxford: Oxford University Press, 2000.

Plutarch, *Plutarch's Greek Lives*. Robin Waterfield, trans. Oxford: Oxford University Press, 1998.

Renault, Mary. *The Nature of Alexander*. New York: Pantheon Books, 1972.

Wood, Michael. *In the Footsteps of Alexander the Great*. Berkeley and Los Angeles: University of California Press, 1997.

Yalouris, Nicholas et al. *The Search for Alexander: An Exhibition*. Boston: New York Graphic Society, 1980.

Fox, Robin Lane. *The Search of Alexander.* Boston: Little, Brown & Company, 1980.

Renault, Mary. *The Nature of Alexander.* New York: Pantheon Books, 1972.

Wood, Michael. *In the Footsteps of Alexander the Great.* Berkeley and Los Angeles: University of California Press, 1997.

Alexander the Great's Home on the Web
http://www.pothos.co.uk/

Alexander the Great on the Web
http://www.isidore-of-seville.com/Alexanderama.html

Alexander the Great History Project
http://www.hackneys.com/alex_web/

Achilles, 49, 79
Acropolis, 35
Afghanistan, 41, 66, 69-73, 95, 98
Aigira, 24
Alexander of Epirus, 23-24
Alexander the Great
    and affect on course of history, 98
    and Afghanistan, 69-73
    and alcohol, 86, 88, 92, 94
    and Bessus, 64-66, 69-70
    birth of, 15
    childhood of, 12-15, 71
    and companions, 38-39, 40, 55, 58,
        64, 67-69, 81, 84, 87, 90, 92-93, 94
    death of, 93-94, 95
    and discontent of army, 66, 67,
        77-79, 91-92
    education of, 18-21, 38
    and Egypt, 50, 52-55, 77, 95
    and evaluation of as conqueror,
        97-98
    family of, 15-16. *See also* Olympias,
        Queen; Philip II, King of Mace-
        donia
    and Greece, 20-21, 22, 24-25, 98-99
    and heroes, 27, 37, 48-49, 77, 79
    and horse, 12-15, 39, 45, 58, 59, 66,
        77, 98
    and India, 15, 54, 70, 73, 74-79,
        80-87, 91, 98
    as king, 24
    as leader, 12-15, 17, 21, 22, 41, 42,
        45-46, 56, 67-69, 77-79, 85, 95-96
    and Persian brides for army, 90
    and Persian Empire, 21, 26-27, 37,
        38-42, 44-47, 48-52, 56-63, 64-65,
        97, 98
    and place in history, 95-99
    and plans to conquer northern
        Europe and Mediterranean,
        94-95
    plot against, 67-69
    as prince, 12-17, 18-22, 24
    as regent, 21
    son of, 95
    and succession, 95
    and tomb of Cyrus the Great, 31,
        88-89
    and wives, 70, 73, 81, 90, 95
    and wounded in India, 82, 85, 86,
        88, 92
Alexandria, 52-53, 95
Ammon of Siwah, 54-55, 56, 77, 91, 95
Amyntas, King (grandfather), 18
Antipater, 26-27, 92, 93, 95
Arabian Desert, 94
Arbela, 59
Aristobulus, 54
Aristotle, 18-21, 38
Arrian, 54, 85, 90
Artaxerxes II, 37
Artazabus, 64
Asia Minor, 22, 31, 32, 33, 34, 35, 37,
    42, 95
Assyrian Empire, 30, 31, 51
Athens, 16, 21, 22, 25, 33-34, 35, 63,
    74, 94, 98
Attic Peninsula, 34, 35

Babylon, 30, 31, 44, 58, 60, 93
Bactria, 31, 34, 41, 56, 58, 64-66,
    69-70, 97-98
Baluchistan, 84
Barbarians, 74, 76
Barsine (wife), 90, 95
Beas River, 91
Bessus, 64-66, 69-70, 73
Black Sea, 37
Bosporus, 38
Bucephalus (city), 77
Bucephalus (horse), 12-15, 39, 45, 58,
    59, 66, 77, 98
Byblus, 48

Callisthenes, 27
Cambyses, 28, 31
Carthage, 50, 94
Caspian Sea, 65, 66
Cassander, 27, 92, 93, 95
Chaldeans, 31

Chareonea, Battle of, 22
Chenab River, 80
Cilician Gates, 44
Civilized peoples, 74, 76
Cleopatra (daughter of Philip), 23-24
Cleopatra (wife of Philip), 22, 24
Cleopatra of Egypt, 22-23, 54
Coenus, 78-79
Corinth, 16, 33
Croesus, King of Lydia, 30
Cyrus II (Cyrus the Great), 28-31, 37,
    41, 60, 62, 83, 84, 88-89
Cyrus the Younger, 37

Damascus, 48, 55
Darius III, 42, 44-47, 48, 55, 56, 58-59,
    62, 64-65, 67, 71, 90, 94
Darius the First (Darius the Great),
    31, 41, 46, 62, 70
Demosthenes, 21
Diodorus, 94
Diogenes, 25
Dionysus, 15, 85

Ecbatana, 30, 31, 60, 62, 67, 93
Egypt
    and Alexander the Great, 50, 52-55,
        77, 95
    and Persian Empire, 31, 41, 53
    and Ptolemies, 53-54, 95
Esther, 60

Fertile Crescent, 30

Gaugamela, Battle of, 56-59, 60, 77
Gaza, 52
Gordian Knot, 42
Gordium, 42
Granicus River, Battle of the, 40-42,
    56
Greece
    and Alexander the Great, 20-21, 22,
        24-25, 98-99
    and Persian Empire, 28, 32-37
    and Philip II, 16-17, 21-22

Halicarnassus, 42
Hebrews, 30, 31
Hellespont (Dardanelles), 27, 34, 35,
    38, 39-40
Hephastion, 38, 40, 45, 71, 73, 74-75,
    90, 91, 92-93, 94
Heracles, 48-49, 77
Herodotus, 20, 27, 31-32, 33-34
Hindu Kush, 66, 69-70
Homer, 27, 40
Hoplites, 33

Illiad (Homer), 40
Immortals, 34
India, 15, 54, 70, 73, 74-79, 80-87,
    91, 98
Indus Delta, 82, 84
Indus River, 75-76, 80-84, 98
Iran, 60, 83-86, 88-89, 97
    See also Persian Empire
Iraq, 56, 97
Issus, Battle of, 44-46, 56, 59, 71, 94, 97

Jerusalem, 30, 52
Jhelum, Battle of the, 76
Jhelum River, 76, 77

Khyber Pass, 73
King's Companions, 22, 41, 45, 59, 67

Lebanon, 51
Leonidas, King of Sparta, 34, 35
Lydians, 30, 31

Macedonia
    army of, 17, 21-22, 38, 41, 58-59,
        67, 69
    and Cassander, 95
    See also Alexander the Great; Philip
        II, King of Macedonia
Makran (Desert of Gedrosia), 34,
    84-85, 90
Marathon, Battle of, 33-34
March of the Ten Thousand, The
    (Xenophon), 37

Marmara, Sea of, 38
Massagetae, 31
Medes, 29-30, 31, 37, 58, 62
Mediterranean Sea, 44, 48, 94
Memphis, 53, 55
Mieza, 20
Monarchy (Aristotle), 20

Nearchus, 84, 87
Nebuchadnezzar, King of Babylon, 30
Nicomachus, 18
Nile Delta, 53
Nile River, 53, 75, 98

Old Testament, 30, 60
Olympias, Queen of Macedonia
    (mother), 15, 16, 17, 20, 22-24, 53,
    54, 71, 92, 93, 95
On Colonies (Aristotle), 20-21
Oxus River, 70, 76, 98

Pakistan, 74, 80, 81, 83, 98
Parmenion, 39, 55, 58, 64, 67-69
Parsa, 60
Parsha, 28, 31
Passeragarde, 31, 60, 62, 88-89
Pella, 15, 18, 20, 25, 65
Persepolis, 60-62, 63, 64, 65, 71, 87, 88
Persian Empire
    and Alexander the Great, 21, 26-27,
        37, 38-42, 44-47, 48-52, 56-63,
        64-65, 97, 98
    and Egypt, 31, 41, 53
    expansion of, 29-34, 37, 62
    and Greece, 28, 32-37
    history of, 28-37
Persian eunuch, 71, 73
Persian Gates, 60-62
Perspolis, 31
Phalanx, 21-22, 41, 44-45, 59-60
Pheidippides, 33, 34
Philip II, King of Macedonia (father),
    12-17, 18-24, 38, 67, 69
    and Alexander as leader, 12-15, 22
    and Alexander as regent, 21

and Alexander's education, 18-21
and Alexander's leadership qualities,
    12-15, 17
assassination of, 24, 46-47
and Greece, 16-17, 21-22
as hostage in Thebes, 17
and Olympias, 15, 16, 17, 20, 22-24,
    71, 92
Philotas, 67, 69
Phoenicians, 31, 35
Pillars of Heracles, 94
Pindar, 25
Plataea, Battle of, 35
Plato, 18
Plutarch, 14, 66
Polis (city-state), 74
Porus, King of the Punjab, 76-77
Poseidon, 82
Postal service (Persian), 31-32
Ptolemies, 53-54, 95
Ptolemy, 39, 53, 95
Punjab, 76, 77
Pyramids, 53

Rock of Sogdiana, 71-72
Roman Empire, 30, 51
Roxanne of Sogdiana (wife), 70, 73,
    81, 95

Sacred Band of Thebes, 22
Salamis, Battle of, 35
Sarmatians, 31
Satrap, 40
Schleiman, Heinrich, 40
Scythians, 70
Semiramas, 83
Sidon, 48, 50
Sindh, 81
Sisygambis, 45-46, 94
Siwah, 54-55, 56, 77, 95
Socrates, 18
Sogdiana, 70-73
Solomon, 30
Sparta, 15, 16, 22, 24, 33, 34-35
Sphinx, 53

Stagira, 18, 19-20
Stateira, 45, 58
Straits of Hormuz, 85-87
Susa, 31, 60, 62, 63, 64, 65, 87, 90

Tajikstan, 66
Thebes, 16, 17, 21, 22, 24-25, 33-34, 51, 97
Themistocles, 35
Thermopylae, 34-35, 61
Trireme vessels, 35
Trojan War, 40, 79
Troy, 40

Turkey. *See* Asia Minor
Tymiris, 31
Tyre, 48-51, 53, 56, 76, 97

Uzbekistan, 66, 70, 95

Victory (city), 77

Xenophon, 27, 28, 37, 41
Xerxes, 34-36, 39-40, 46, 60, 62

Zeus, 82

page:

2: TK
13: Scala/Art Resource, NY
16: Giraudon/Art Resource, NY
19: Hulton Archive/Getty Images
23: Scala/Art Resource, NY
26: Hierophant Collection
29: Dave Bartuff/CORBIS
32: Hulton Archive/Getty Images
36: Hierophant Collection
39: Hierophant Collection
43: North Carolina Museum of Art/
    CORBIS
46: Roger Wood/CORBIS
49: Bettmann/CORBIS
52: Peter M. Wilson/CORBIS

55: Reunion des Musees Nationaux/
    Art Resource, NY
57: Giraudon/Art Resource, NY
61: Hierophant Collection
65: Ric Ergenbright/CORBIS
68: Scala/Art Resource, NY
72: Hierophant Collection
75: Reunion des Musees Nationaux/
    Art Resource, NY
78: Bettmann/CORBIS
81: Lloyd Cluff/CORBIS
83: CORBIS
86: Bettmann/CORBIS
89: Tate Gallery, London/Art Resource, NY
96: Bettmann/CORBIS

Cover: Erich Lessing/Art Resource, NY
Frontis: Scala/Art Resource, NY

SAMUEL WILLARD CROMPTON has a deep interest in the Classical world of Greece and Rome. He has written *Gods and Goddesses of Classical Mythology* as well as *100 Military Leaders Who Shaped World History* and *100 Battles that Shaped World History*. Mr. Crompton teaches both American History and Western Civilization at Holyoke Community College in Massachusetts. He has twice served as a Writing Fellow for Oxford University Press in its production of the 24-volume *American National Biography*. He has written several other books with Chelsea House, including *Waterloo, Hastings,* and *Tenochtitlan.*

ARTHUR M. SCHLESINGER, JR. is the leading American historian of our time. He won the Pulitzer Prize for his book *The Age of Jackson* (1945) and again for a chronicle of the Kennedy Administration, *A Thousand Days* (1965), which also won the National Book Award. Professor Schlesinger is the Albert Schweitzer Professor of the Humanities at the City University of New York and has been involved in several other Chelsea House projects, including the series REVOLUTIONARY WAR LEADERS, COLONIAL LEADERS, and YOUR GOVERNMENT.